GW00383068

Start Backpacking

Also by Mike Marriott

Desert Taxi
Two Up to Australia
The Handbook for Motor Cyclists
Caravanning with BP
Scooter Care
Car Camping in Spain
Car Camping in Switzerland
Car Camping in Italy
Boys' Book of Racing and Sports Cars
The Pennine Way Long Distance Path
The South West Peninsular Path

Mike Marriott

Start Backpacking

Stanley Paul
London Melbourne Sydney Auckland Johannesburg

Stanley Paul & Co. Ltd

An imprint of the Hutchinson Publishing Group

3 Fitzroy Square, London W1P 6JD

Hutchinson Group (Australia) Pty Ltd
30-32 Cremorne Street, Richmond South, Victoria 3121
PO Box 151, Broadway, New South Wales 2007

Hutchinson Group (NZ) Ltd
32-34 View Road, PO Box 40-086, Glenfield, Auckland 10

Hutchinson Group (SA) Pty Ltd
PO Box 337, Bergvlei 2012, South Africa

First published 1981

© Mike Marriott 1981

The paperback edition of this book is sold subject to the
condition that it shall not, by way of trade or otherwise,
be lent, re-sold, hired out or otherwise circulated in any
form of binding or cover other than that in which it is
published and without a similar condition including this
condition being imposed on the subsequent purchaser

Set in Intertype Plantin

Printed in Great Britain by The Anchor Press Ltd
and bound by Wm Brendon & Son Ltd,
both of Tiptree, Essex

British Library Cataloguing in Publication Data
Marriott, Mike
    Start backpacking.
    1. Backpacking
    I. Title
    796.5'1   GV199.6

ISBN 0 09 143990 6 cased
       0 09 143991 4 paper

The author wishes to thank Karrimor, Berghaus,
and Bantan & Co. for help in supplying some of
the illustrations for this book and the publishers to
thank the Countryside Commission for the use of the
map on pages 80 and 81

Contents

Foreword

When anyone mentions backpacking, the image I get is one of adventure – that feeling of heading out into the unknown – and the freedom it conjures up. It takes me back about a decade or so to a few trips I too made with the author, Mike Marriott, when backpacking was just beginning to take-off in the United Kingdom.

At that time I had already known Mike for around ten years, when he introduced me to snow camping and the wonderful satisfaction gained by setting oneself against the elements in winter. Subsequent sorties included winter walks in Snowdonia and south coastal jaunts without so much as a tent – sleeping-out in all a frosty night could offer as a challenge.

But even before I knew him, he had already established himself as an adventurous traveller and author, when in the early fifties, he and his wife crossed the Sahara in nothing more elaborate than an ancient London taxi, to be followed by a second overland trip to Australia – on a scooter.

So if anyone at all should be writing about the great outdoors and backpacking, it should be Mike Marriott. Although the activity originated in America, it would be true to say that he has always been a pioneer in this country. As a regular contributor to the camping press, he has done much to stimulate interest and bring the sport to what it is today. Much of the sophisticated equipment now available is due to practical research he has carried out and more than one piece carries his name.

This book is written in an authoritative manner and contains a wealth of information for the beginner. The early chapters are of special importance, for here the author deals in great depth with the large selection of equipment now available, and puts special emphasis on getting the priorities right. Later chapters then deal with actually taking to the road and here, too, his expertise stresses the need to start humbly and work up to the more arduous trips when experience has been gained. Only by so doing can the beginner avoid discouragement when problems are encountered. The book must surely be an essential item in the kit of every newcomer to backpacking.

Eric Fowler
Information Officer,
The Camping Club of Great Britain
and Ireland.

Author's Preface

When the Publishers first asked me to write this book, they did so with some reservations. Were we not, perhaps, flooding the market? I too had my doubts at first about the validity of a further title on the subject of back-packing.

There *are* a number of excellent beginners guides available by established and esteemed writers like Derek Booth, Peter Lumley and Robin Adshead (see section on further reading), and I strongly recommend you to read them and indeed, any others you can lay hands on.

For the simple truth is that in order to extract the utmost from this particular pursuit, you really cannot have too much knowledge. Being the highly personalized exercise that it is, you will get some very personal opinions from each author, on what constitutes the best in backpacking.

Information overlap there will surely be, but emphasis will differ and if some views about equipment or technique seem diametrically opposed, so much the better. The end result should be not a copy-book follower of this writer or that, but an informed participant strong on *self*-reliance; a virtue that is crucial to those who seek the best in backpacking . . .

Chapter One
First Steps

The American word 'backpacking' may sound ugly but it describes succinctly the subject of this book: the art of self-propelled, self-contained travel.

Basically, backpacking is a mixture of hiking and camping and certainly it owes much to these popular pursuits. In practice, however, it is far more than this. It is a singularly specialized and immensely satisfying game with a character all its own. Addictive enough to become not only a pastime but a positive way of life.

The original backpacker – practising the art for survival rather than leisure – was probably the North American Indian. It was he who discovered that an H-shaped frame of birchwood lashed with rawhide thongs and harnessed to his back could transport not only animal pelts but personal possessions too. Thus he could travel comfortably and efficiently, leaving hands free (for bow and arrow, presumably), and with little or no impediment to the basic business of putting one foot before the other. The North American Indian was followed, of course, by generations of European trappers who roamed the vast network of wilderness trails in Canada and North America for months – even seasons – on end, fully mobile, yet with their homes literally on their backs.

Little wonder then that the backpack evolved as the accepted method of transporting possessions across rugged country throughout the world. Modified, modernized, it became, in one form or another, the life-support system for countless other people: prospectors, hunters, explorers and every army ever raised.

A Lake District landscape. Typical terrain for winter backpacking

Checking the weight and balance of the pack before setting off

Foot soldiers could seldom be heard singing the praises of the dead weight on their shoulders, but there was no efficient alternative.

And so it is today – though the backpack and its contents have changed beyond recognition. New thinking about design, materials, methods of production and field application have spurred manufacturers to heights of imaginative creation undreamed of a couple of decades ago. The result is a magic formula which makes walking with a pack a true pleasure rather than a masochistic chore, by providing vastly increased efficiency of equipment coupled with drastically reduced weight and bulk.

Where our predecessor hiker/camper was burdened with huge loads often weighing up to 60 pounds or more, the modern backpacker presents by comparison a slimline profile. His pack weighs a mere 20 to 30 pounds, and the equipment within ensures him of home-from-home comforts in any climate from arctic to equatorial, and in any location from the New Forest to the slopes of the Himalayas.

The significance of these developments will not be lost on those of independent spirit who love the outdoor life and the freedom of open sky country. The potential is wide indeed. Backpacking can be – and is – enjoyed by all age groups, both sexes, individually and gregariously, over every kind of terrain, and at all seasons of the year.

At its simplest, it is a gentle weekend stroll along, perhaps, a 10 mile stretch of National Trust footpath, an overnight pitch in a friendly farm paddock and a return walk to the car next day. For the veteran aficionado, on the other hand, backpacking may mean a trip lasting months and entailing a marathon trek from the English Channel to the Mediterranean, or the length of the Appalachian trail in America.

Between the two extremes, there are footpath miles to explore in Britain alone which would take several lifetimes to cover. The Pennine Way, the South-West Peninsula Path and Offa's Dyke are just three long-distance routes among many awaiting those ready and willing to discover, or rediscover, that their legs are not just for operating car pedals.

What then is the fascination of this fast-growing leisure activity? Well, firstly backpacking is exciting and full of adventure, but it holds few of the dangers of climbing, small-boat sailing and the like. There are hazards, to be sure – enough to keep the senses keenly honed – but seldom, if ever, the sudden and serious dangers associated with many other outdoor sports. Hence the backpacker may be any age between eight or eighty. So long as he or she is relatively fit, the portals are open. Once begun and practised regularly, backpacking not only makes you fitter but keeps you that way. It is an outdoor game that may be pursued for a lifetime.

This group may look cheerful, but their packs will be too low for comfort by the end of the day

Backpacking provides many different pleasures. Perhaps most importantly, it stretches you physically in a very beneficial way – a vital antidote to the sedentary daily life which most of us have to endure. It takes you into countryside never seen from the car window and makes you aware of your natural surroundings as no mechanized travel can do.

Backpacking exercises the intellect too, since a certain amount of route finding with map and compass is often needed, and it certainly sharpens self-reliance and stimulates ingenuity – if only to find a cosy and congenial pitch as dusk gathers.

Deeper fulfilment comes from the knowledge that you are living simply, close to the good earth, not upsetting the ecology, and burning no fossil fuel. Travelling in fact much as nature intended, yet with space-age aids

A party of novice backpackers setting out

providing all the creature comforts to make each journey self-sufficient as well as a voyage of discovery.

It is hardly necessary to stress the import-ance of natural breaks to punctuate our frenetic workaday existence in the concrete jungle. As a foil to grossly artificial living conditions, backpacking offers something natural and fresh.

Be it a mere weekend, a fortnight or a month, almost every minute is spent under the open sky. The good this does to heart, lungs and limbs – and psyche – cannot be bought. The gentle but sustained exercise of distance walking is the best body toner there is (apart possibly from swimming) and, coupled with

society why on earth should anyone want to load themselves like pack mules and *walk* across country for fun? Only those who did it knew the answer and they were quite content to keep it to themselves.

Then, quite abruptly, the sport took off. The take-off was fuelled by the camping press which was only reflecting new social attitudes: a growing disenchantment with the car; an awareness that a spreading waistline and a surfeit of TV do not equate with happiness; and a desire for more adventurous pursuits than beach lazing and traditional camping.

There was a growing hunger to return to the countryside and *do* something with precious leisure time, in order to feel – at least occasionally – fully alive. That hunger was assuaged by backpacking. Now, like cycling, it is enjoying a renaissance which would have seemed inconceivable twenty-odd years ago. 'Backpacking' is already a household word with a place in every new dictionary, and there is an established National Backpackers Club and a whole host of specialist retailers to help you get the right equipment. This is important because the choice of contemporary light-weight camping gear, the backpacks themselves, boots, clothing and auxiliaries, is so wide as to be almost totally bewildering to the tyro.

Backpackers are often great individualists, and one of the virtues of backpacking is that it is a thinking person's sport, continually challenging the participant, goading him or her to extract just that little more from their chosen equipment in the interests of efficiency or comfort, testing personal stamina and making them perceptibly more adventurous each time out.

In this book, however, we are concerned strictly with basics and we will leave experiment to the more experienced. The purpose of this book, as the title plainly suggests, is to tell you how to *start* backpacking smoothly and to help you avoid some common pitfalls. I hope in the following pages at least to open the door to a fascinating, specialized pursuit which dedicated enthusiasts describe, quite simply, as the best in the world.

the challenge of ultra-lightweight camping, it recharges the batteries far more efficiently and for much longer than the most frantic gym work-out or jog around the local park.

Little more than a decade ago, when most people thought petrol would remain cheap and plentiful, backpacking was very much a minority sport. And one for an eccentric if not lunatic minority at that. In a car-oriented

Chapter Two
Basic Equipment

At the very start of this book, we are faced with a dilemma. As the late Professor Joad used to declaim, 'It all depends on what you mean by basic.' The word can – and does – have totally different connotations for the eager yet impoverished student on the one hand, and the affluent middle-aged executive on the other.

It would be presumptuous of me to proffer dogmatic advice about choice of equipment. So much depends on aspiration, physical attributes, finances available and so on. What I can do is to indicate all the *proven* alternatives of basic walking and lightweight camping gear, from which you (who certainly know yourself better than anyone) can short-list the most suitable. Bear in mind then that these alternatives are flexible and that cross-pollination is often beneficial.

Firstly though I should dispel some of the mystique that has grown around equipment for backpacking. Despite the high levels of sophistication that have been reached, it is no bad thing to keep the fundamental objective firmly in mind. You are equipping yourself to walk for *fun*.

This can be done with the most frugal of gear – indeed, with almost no special equipment at all, provided prudence tempers enthusiasm. Far better then to make do with the minimum in the early days than to let the tail swing the cat. Try to avoid becoming an equipment freak. The man with the most gear not only spends the most, but often walks the least. Talking about those with the most, if you are affluent and interested in backpacking, you can walk into the nearest specialist store,

A correctly loaded and balanced pack (right)
and the dramatic cliffs at Durdle Door

equip yourself completely and set off at once for the hills. And good luck.

Most of us, however, have to approach the kitting-out process with more financial caution. It is wise to think carefully before making any major purchase and the average newcomer frequently spends the whole of his first season getting the complete outfit together. You have to start somewhere though, and this raises the question of priorities. Which major item comes first: pack, tent, boots, clothing, sleeping bag?

My recommendation, which I would stress is personal, would be to opt for the footwear. Especially if you fall within that vast band of people who, up till now anyway, only walk when they have to. The time between buying the boots and the next piece of equipment may then be usefully employed in preparing those over-softened feet for some serious walking.

Backpacking means independence from closed or fully booked hotels

Much depends on age, pocket and physical condition, of course, and what may be quite acceptable to a hardy teenager may prove disastrous to an overweight grandfather. There are no hard and fast rules about what you should wear on your feet, despite the claims of the overcautious safety lobby.

There are young tigers who wear nothing stouter than lightweight training boots, whatever the season or terrain, seemingly immune to wet feet and blisters. Others, who cannot tolerate restriction around the ankles, opt for stout walking shoes. Women often find these favourable. Some ex-army types are quite happy in ammo boots, and a minority even tramp blissfully in plastic or rubber wellies – the only footwear, incidentally, that is totally waterproof.

Here, however, we are concerned with the accepted norm, which means the orthodox, natural leather hill-walking boot. Nowadays the market is largely dominated by Italy and, in the quality ranges at least, Italian boots are

excellent value for money. The Swiss and Austrians also build fine boots, as do one or two British companies like Hawkins. There is no question, though, that for comfort, weather-proofing, durability and style, the Italian walking boot has few peers.

Scarpa (the name means 'shoe' in Italian) is just one popular make, Robusta another: two companies producing between them three models highly popular with backpackers. All are cut in more or less one-piece leather (ensuring the minimum of stitching and hence the maximum of proofing), all are double skinned and strategically padded, all have sewn-in tongues to keep puddle water at bay.

At the lower end of the price range, the Sella is the least complex. Constructed from a beautifully supple leather, it is a favourite with both sexes, for it gives good ankle support yet is light in weight – hardly heavier than a

Right: The old-fashioned, heavily studded walking boot

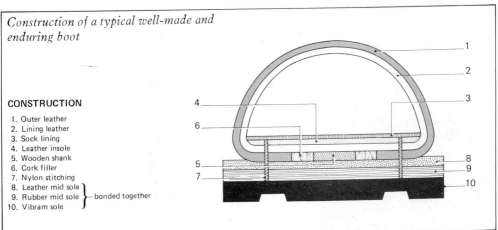

Construction of a typical well-made and enduring boot

CONSTRUCTION

1. Outer leather
2. Lining leather
3. Sock lining
4. Leather insole
5. Wooden shank
6. Cork filler
7. Nylon stitching
8. Leather mid sole ⎫
9. Rubber mid sole ⎬ bonded together
10. Vibram sole ⎭

Table of English and continental shoe sizes

CONTINENTAL SIZE:	26	27	28	29	30	31	32	33	34	35	36	37
ENGLISH EQUIVALENT:	—	—	—	—	—	—	—	—	2	2¾	3½	4½

CONTINENTAL SIZE:	38	39	40	41	42	43	44	45	46	47	48
ENGLISH EQUIVALENT:	5	5¾	6½	7¼	8	8¾	9½	10¼	11	11¾	12½

pair of walking shoes. This is achieved partly by using an impact-adhesive sole/heel direct to the upper. They are repairable, but only with difficulty. Really a day-walking boot (as opposed to a true hill-walking model), it is none the less excellent for high-summer walking and/or with an ultra-lightweight pack.

Whilst any number of people *do* wear Sellas and comparable models, even with the heaviest of backpacks, most enthusiasts opt eventually for something rather more sturdy. The Trento is, I think, justly famed as one of the best medium-priced backpacking boots available.

This is manufactured from the same supple leather as the Sella, but there the resemblance ends. The Trento is altogether chunkier, more robust and therefore heavier – though not excessively so. Its big feature is the 'shanked' sole – a strategic stiffening of the instep with a hickory wedge inserted between sole and upper to prevent overflexing. The one-piece sole and heel is made of commando-pattern

The Sella boot

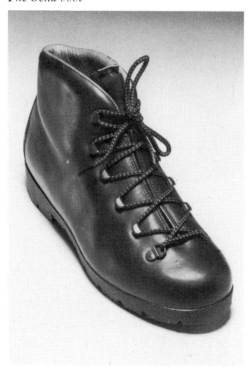

Vibram, one of the hardest wearing composites available.

The boot has superb non-slip properties on most surfaces, and the makers term this pattern 'self-shedding', i.e. cloggy mud tends to work outwards, worm-like, as you walk. A true virtue this, when you are struggling through glutinous mud – otherwise the boots may easily become twice as heavy as usual.

Between the commando sole and upper leather, there is a leather sub-sole; these layers are joined by a high-pressure adhesive system, without visible screws or stitching. To repair, the sole-and-heel piece is removed entirely from the leather platform and a new one impacted. Apart from a central heel strip, the upper is one piece and there is an internal toe block for protective rigidity. Lacing is via a pair of closed eyes at the toe end and thence by open cleats.

Third choice in the range is the Brenta, which is really a deluxe version of the Trento. Slightly higher grade leather is used here, and the boot has a more luxuriously padded and 'hinged' tongue, as well as closed-eye lacing instead of open cleats (save at the ankle), a crimped leather closure band around the ankle top and extra screw fastening through the heel plates.

There is a fourth, super-deluxe alternative: the Bronzo. This boot is built from the finest chrome leather and the uppers really are one piece, with just a single stitch line running from ankle top to heel. The uppers are not only impacted to the soles but are also screwed and stitched. The result is a boot designed to cope with the roughest and wettest terrain and o go on doing it almost indefinitely. Also something of a dual-purpose model, the Bronzo can be worn for rock scrambling (as opposed to purist climbing), as well as backpacking.

The drawback to these boots, apart from the price, is their weight (somewhere in the region of 6 pounds a pair) and, for all but specialist walkers, or those with a 16 to 18 stone physique, they are often too substantial.

These then are three fairly different kinds of boot from just two quality stables. There are others equally favoured by the backpack-

Above: *The Brenta boot.*
Right: *The Bronzo boot*

ing fraternity. Whatever your personal
selection, it probably will not differ drastically
in specification from those described here.

Quality hill-walking boots are expensive
and, whilst I would urge you to buy the best
you can afford in the interests of efficiency,
comfort and safety, a word must be said about
cheaper expedients. Students with thinly lined
pockets and those even younger whose feet are
still growing need not be too discouraged.

Top-quality boots are highly desirable but
not absolutely essential in the early stages,
provided the wearer is conscious of their
limitations. If funds are limited, you might
consider pattern-soled walking boots from
Czechoslovakia, the better type of home-
produced work boot, or even the leisure boot
often available at surplus stores.

Search around for boots similar to the
quality models described here and, when you
have found something in the economy range
that you think may fit the bill, check carefully

to make sure the construction is sturdy. The uppers should be leather and not plastic (not always easy to detect), but if in doubt your nose should be able to sniff out the real thing.

The four salient requirements of any back-packing boot – from the cheapest to the highest-priced bespoke – are: substantial insulation between your foot and the ground; a non-slip sole; good ankle support; and, of course, efficient weather-resistant properties.

Whatever the final selection of footwear, it is vitally important that the fit is as near perfect as possible. When you walk for a prolonged period your feet expand as nature intended, often considerably. And the process is accelerated when you are carrying a 20 or 30 pound load on your back.

In order to compensate for this foot spreading, you must think oversize. One number up from normal shoe fitting is about right. The initial 'cold fit' surplus is then taken up by extra socks. Not dress socks in this case, but the thick Norwegian ragg-wool variety – standard with nearly all hill walkers and climbers.

As a general rule, one pair of nylon under-socks (cotton if the feet are ultra-sensitive), plus the ragg socks will be sufficient, though there are exceptions. The ankle-length type are the most popular but, if you suffer from

A well-made boot should have a sole indented like this

cold legs, intend doing a lot of winter walking, or favour plus-two climbing breeches, knee-length oversocks may be preferred.

The specialist retailer should advise you expertly on boot fitting and he should also supply trial socks for the purpose. If you are left to your own devices, here is a good rule-of-thumb guide to fitting. With the boot *unlaced* and your foot thrust well forward into the toe end, you should be able to slip your index finger *fairly easily* between your heel and the rear boot wall.

Now, with the boots securely but not brutally laced, stand up, flex yourself a bit and start walking up and down the shop. The first steps, particularly if you are unused to boots (and you have opted for a shanked model), will be a mite strange. You may even feel like a cross between a deep-sea diver and Franken-stein's monster.

It is this very feature that will later ensure tireless comfort when you get into the hills. Back and forth then, and if all goes well you should detect the subtle change in walking technique within five minutes or so. The shanked boot tends to make you walk slightly slower and more deliberately, with a definite heel-down-first action. Curiously, often after a very short time, this becomes perfectly natural and you simply do not notice the tell-tale double clump as each step is taken. This disappears entirely once the boot has 'broken' and taken on that characteristic slightly

upturned shape. During the trial walk you will of course be testing for comfort. There should be ample room (though not an obvious excess) to flex all your toes and absolutely no suspicion of tightness along the outer sides of the boots or across the instep. A slight amount of heel lift is permissible; indeed, it is sometimes unavoidable with brand new shanked boots, but extra tightening of the laces should eliminate most of the movement after one or two wearings. This in turn may cause a slight discomfort around the ankle. Be assured though that this is merely a temporary irritant. Ankle skin is usually sensitive and women especially sometimes suffer ankle chafe at first. This, I repeat, will disappear totally and permanently after a short while.

If this is a trouble spot during the early days, simply drop the laces down one cleat to get relief, but lace fully again as soon as possible since tight laces provide so much of that essential ankle support. After five or ten minutes of shop walking, you should know beyond doubt if your final choice is the right one. But I would emphasize that this walking exercise is crucial. Ten seconds of stamping up and down on the spot may be all right for dress shoes but it is not sufficient when you are selecting backpacking boots.

Here I must add a rider about socks to help the man or woman who has, for want of a better description, non-standard feet. Quite a few people have real trouble finding foot comfort for everyday walking, let alone for long-distance tramping. Do remember that there are many different ways of using socks. You can wear one, two or three pairs of socks, or even two socks on one foot and three on the other – a ploy which is often very successful if you know one foot is slightly larger than the other. You can remove one pair of socks if your feet have expanded after a few miles. You can also employ aerated or lambswool insoles and ensure blister-free progress by using a preventative deer-fat application. By way of encouragement at this point, the more you walk the easier it becomes. You will find more about socks and foot comfort later.

Do not hurry, though, to convert those brand new boots into familiar friends.

Breaking-in should be a leisurely procedure. This is one reason why footwear is discussed first. Whilst you are saving for the next major item – the pack – you can wear the boots casually yet frequently at home, perhaps to work, or to explore all those local footpaths you hardly knew existed.

This is the painless way to transform those shiny and seemingly ungiving objects into snug-fitting faithfuls. Walking not only prepares the boots for their ultimate purpose in the best possible manner, it also does the same for your no doubt tender feet. Do *not* be tempted by drastic break-in methods like overnight immersion of boots in the bath, using hot melted dubbin or beating with a mallet as you would a tough steak. Contemporary walking boots are half broken in anyway when compared with what they used to be, and such treatment is more likely to break them up than break them in.

When you get them home apply a generous coating of a preservative like Kiwi Wetprufe. If you do use preparations like dubbin or Mars Oil, which are designed to soften the tougher leather-like cowhide and so on used in horse harnesses, be very sparing. Italian boot leather is already supple and needs only a modicum of extra dressing. If you use too much oil or dubbin there is a risk of over-softening the boots. You then lose much of the ankle support they are supposed to provide and any stitching is overlubricated to the point where it begins to work. Enlarged stitch-holes and subsequent water letting may result.

Coat liberally the first time, working the wax in with your fingers rather than a cloth, paying particular attention to that line across the front of the upper where the leather will eventually 'break'. Leave overnight, then brush off the tacky surplus next morning. Repeat the process in a week or ten days and thereafter *not more* than six times annually, unless the boots are worked very hard under prolonged wet conditions.

One or two useful tips now to ensure you extract long and faithful service from these, the most important items in your backpacking outfit. Always dry them naturally, never in front of a fire or on a radiator. If you must

speed the process, do so with a loose stuffing of newspaper, or soft toilet tissue, which is even more absorbent.

Acid is the greatest enemy of leather, so at the end of any day walking through whisky-coloured water so typical of peat country, do wash your boots thoroughly. Fresh gin-coloured water (to continue the booze analogy) is what is needed, even if this means sloshing through a running stream or rain puddles.

Keep the commando soles clear of clogging by removing flints, small stones or stubborn mud as soon as convenient. And finally, do not leave it too late for repairs or the vital leather sub-sole, to which the new sole must be attached, may be damaged. When the heel is patently worn down and the sole tread is too shallow to hold small stone chips or footpath debris, the boot needs repairing. Exactly when, in terms of time or miles, this stage is likely to be reached is somewhat difficult to assess. It depends of course on how frequently the boots are worn, the weight and walking action of the wearer, the amount of roadwork involved (the quickest way to wear out boots), and the general maintenance (or lack of it).

One person may wear out his boots in a single season, another might manage seven years or more on the original tread pattern. Five years is about *average*. In which case you may reasonably expect to get ten years of total life.

This should encourage you to go initially for quality regardless, within reason, of cost. There is absolutely nothing more confidence building to the walker than donning a pair of sturdy, well-fitting boots which will carry him efficiently across the most broken, wet or slippery terrain.

If the choice of walking boots is wide, that of backpacks is even more difficult and frequently very confusing to the newcomer. So once again I want to simplify the situation by listing the basic models that have earned themselves a

In this kind of terrain good boots are essential, especially when moving downhill

good track record. You will make your own mind up about what suits you best, but by now you should have a reasonable idea of what constitutes a functional, robust and, most importantly, comfortable backpack.

I should like to start by suggesting a couple of models for serious backpackers to avoid. There are countless rucksack wanderers who are *not* backpackers in the true sense, who carry a pack in order to hitch-hike, etc. For this kind of travel long-term pack durability and comfort are not so important. So beware the cheap imitation – the model ostensibly like the quality article, yet often half its price. Look a little closer at that bargain from the Far East, for example, and you will probably find that the material lacks body and is far from waterproof; the stitching may be poor, the zips and closures on pockets rough and rudimentary. Attachment of sack to frame may be flimsy, the frame or strap attachments may buckle or break after a short time.

For physical comfort you should also steer clear of the old-fashioned Bergan-type ruck-sack. Although they are often beautifully made, the weight of the cotton duck pack itself, with its tubular built-in steel frame and chrome-leather fittings is, to say the least, off-putting. When packed, the loading is too low and concentrated on the back. Briefly, the differ-ence between this and the modern backpack is like the difference between a leaf-sprung car and one with independent suspension.

Enough of negative advice. Let's consider genuine backpacker choice. Despite a host of makes and models there are just *two* basic units. The framed high pack and the somewhat newer but already popular ergonomic or anatomic backpack. It is necessary, in order to give you some idea of what to look for, to examine both in some detail.

The high pack consists essentially of two parts: an aluminium H-shaped frame and a capacious sack of man-made fibre which is attached independently. The frame itself may be open-shaped at the bottom (like the letter H) or 'booted' to form a cross-member base platform. Both types are equally popular. There is less metal and fractionally less weight

In bushy or wooded terrain a narrow pack soon proves its worth

with the former, but the booted frame stands easier, keeps the sack base off the ground and provides a housing (depending on sack size), for a stuff-sack, about which more later.

In profile the frame is cunningly shaped to conform to the contours of the human back and it is held together by plastic and screw compression joints or arc welding. The first method is less expensive and is preferred by some since it is easy to repair, provided the owner is equipped with a spare joint and screw and a suitable star screwdriver – an advantage should the frame be damaged or broken miles from anywhere. It is a good idea, by the way, to check the tightness of the frame screws periodically.

The arc-welded frame has many advantages and maintains constant rigidity under all conditions, no matter, within reason, how heavy the load. The welded frame should give a life-time of service with virtually no maintenance. The only difficulty is repairing if the welded frame should be accidentally damaged.

Attached to the basic frame are the shoulder straps via rings and pins or short nylon straps, and lateral spacer bands cushion the wearer's back against the metal of the frame. On some screw-jointed models the position of the top cross-bar can be changed, and extra screw holes through the side frames are provided for this purpose. Since all quality units are available in different sizes to suit individual back lengths, this is not imperative. Alteration of the cross-bar position is not of course possible with arc-welded frames. On most models straps can also be adjusted to cope with different shoulder widths.

When high packs first came on to the market the padded hip-belt was seen as something of a luxury extra. Nowadays it is rightly considered a standard part of the top-quality outfit. Once nothing more than a strap to prevent the backpack bumping about, it is now a super-luxury device which not only keeps the pack figure-hugging at all times, but actually transfers the *major loading* of the whole pack from the shoulders to the pelvis.

What this means in terms of comfort and tireless extended walking is better experienced

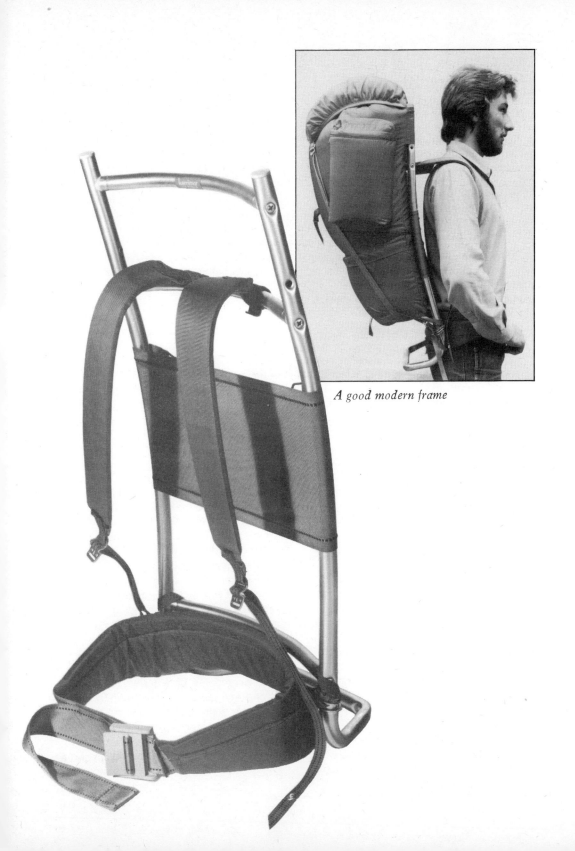

A good modern frame

than described. Anyone who has ever struggled along with an old-style pack with the shoulder straps cutting ever deeper will know what I mean.

Indeed, the framed pack, hip-belted firmly in position, tends to make the wearer walk almost *more* upright than is normal with no pack at all – rather than bowed over thumbing desperately at chafing straps. The benefit of this upright stance is immense.

On to the frame goes the sack, again attached by rings and pins or straps. In its simplest form, this is a straight-through nylon sack with a deep flap held by cord and rings or straps and buckles. Covering virtually the length of the frame and tapered in profile to provide a narrow base and wide top, it enables the contents to be distributed over the whole of the wearer's back from the nape of the neck to the hip line in the most efficient way possible.

Advantages of the simple straight-through sack are: ease of packing, relatively low initial price, no extraneous weight of pockets, zips and so on. Even though this extra weight might only amount to a few grams, it is an important saving to many enthusiasts.

One other argument for the pocketless sack – appreciated by those who like to hill walk among the higher peaks and combine back-packing with the odd spot of rock scrambling – there are no projecting pockets to slow progress when the track narrows. However, a framed pack should never be used for serious climbing, since the frame itself could snag dangerously on any tricky rock face.

This is of minority interest though and most backpackers prefer the compartmented, pocketed sack. Top of the popularity list comes the unit with the following specification: a total carrying capacity of around 60 to 70 litres (the standard measurement method adopted by all major manufacturers). The main compartment is divided halfway down by a sewn-in floor panel, but with corner holes at the rear to give full-length access for tent poles. This base section is reachable separately via a frontal zip or zips. Capacious side pockets are provided, two on each side with deluxe models, often with rear-facing zip

closures to make access possible without shedding the pack.

A large, square, boxed pocket, again with rear zip on quality models, graces the top of the main flap, which in turn may incorporate or conceal (sewn into the front wall) a document compartment with a zip or Velcro fastener. There will probably be a snow-sleeve extension of slightly thinner material sewn to the top of the main opening, sealing off both by means of drawstrings and quick-action cord-locks.

The front flap has widely varying closure positions to accommodate different loads, and it often has an elasticated edging for increased weatherproofing; there will probably be a lifting loop at the top and one or two external attachment loops.

The material will be of internally coated waterproof nylon (7 ounce fabric or there-abouts), or the new Cordura which, though totally man-made, is a fairly good simulation of the more characterful canvas.

There are two other features often incor-porated into top-quality frame sacks which are of interest to rock scramblers or to the growing clan of keen winter ski walkers. On models like the Karrimor Totem Senior, for instance, it is possible to use the sack without the frame. This is achieved through the use of an optional extra U-tube which is inserted in place of the full frame. Shoulder straps are then secured in the normal manner. The result is an effective, if temporary, frameless rucksack.

Other models may have detachable side pockets, again optional, increasing overall capacity to cope for example with winter equipment extras or those needed for a prolonged trip. The resulting gap between pockets and main sack is ideal for stowing short walking skis, and some manufacturers provide this feature as standard even where pockets are permanently sewn.

The ergonomic pack derives its name from physics and was coined in Britain by the Karrimor boffins. This type of pack is the result of adapting a backpack to the human form in the most efficient way possible. An ergon, by the way, is 'a measurement of the work done by a unit of force on a body which moves in the direction of action of the force'. If, like me, you find this baffling, never mind the description, feel the pack.

There is no question that the advent of this ergonomic or anatomic backpack has heralded another big leap forward in the business of pedestrian load-carrying. Basically, the capacity, layout and number of sections and pockets does not differ drastically from the externally framed pack, though the ergonomic is, as a rule, fractionally smaller and narrower. Where it does depart distinctly is in the body-hugging design achieved through small-diameter or even flat internal framing and a very substantial built-in hip-belt system. Once hefted on to the shoulders and secured, the well-fitting anatomic pack becomes an almost integral part of the walker, virtually immovable no matter how strenuous the walking. It is, as a result, very comfortable.

Again, though, this asset must be qualified. Provided the all-up load does not exceed about 25 pounds, the walker of standard build could hardly do better than use an internally framed ergonomic pack, and this makes it a very attractive proposition from spring through to autumn when conditions are mild and the backpacking equipment light. In typical winter conditions (which can of course be experienced in areas like the Lake District and the Cairngorms during almost any month), when a heavier pack has perforce to be carried, the externally framed pack may well be preferred, especially when the pack tips the scales at over the 35 pound mark. If the load is nearer 40 pounds, the framed high pack is almost obligatory for those of average physique.

There is one other consideration which may be more important to some than others: many ergonomic packs are very close fitting. Indeed this is a major part of their attraction. However, for those who sweat with healthy freedom, the proximity of pack to back may mean a constantly soaked shirt or pullover. In some cases this discomfort can prove unacceptable. Some makers are now producing packs which are slightly less figure hugging and this does go some way to solving the problem. The Karrimor Aergo models are

A body-hugging backpack

examples. I must emphasize that only a minority of users are seriously affected, but it is a point to bear in mind. In any case, all quality anatomic packs have a natural cotton buffer preventing direct body contact with nylon. Further elimination of excess sweat can be had by wearing a thermal vest, which is discussed in a later chapter.

Another advantage of the anatomic unit is that it is super snug on a cold day when a constantly warm back is pure delight. Under such weather conditions, though, can you keep equipment weight around that 25 pound maximum?

If all these pros and cons are beginning to confuse you, I did say that backpacking is a thinker's sport! There is perhaps no such thing as the perfect all-round backpack; and if and when the bug bites deeply enough you may well wind up with a couple of alternative units.

Be that as it may, we are here concerned that your first choice is the best pack for your specific and immediate needs. Despite the apparent difficulty of choice, I trust you are

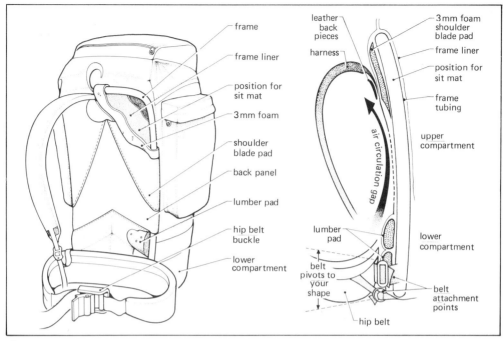

Anatomy of a semi-body-hugging backpack

now more familiar with the alternatives and thus more confident about your final selection.

The first practical move, then, is to visit an equipment shop, and I recommend that you choose a specialist supplier of lightweight gear, rather than a general store. Lists of these will be found in all the recognized camping and outdoor-life magazines. You will find a selection of further reading at the end of the book.

You may have to travel some distance from home, for such specialists are fairly thin on the ground in Great Britain, but the effort should reap its own reward. After sampling the fit of both framed and ergonomic packs, you should have a pretty good idea which best suits your ambition, temperament and pocket.

The dealer who caters for the enthusiast will have sandbags or similar of various weights which can be inserted into the pack to give simulated equipment loads. Whilst this is a very good test method, it is not *always* infallible. Here again, the really concerned retailer will allow you to buy on approval. Exchange, though, should rarely be necessary.

As a rule, provided you know more or less what you are after, the dealer will ensure you choose a pack that fits your back precisely.

With the frame pack it is usual to select a correctly sized frame to which the standard pack is then matched. There are, though, some designs where both frame and pack are variable. As a yardstick, when the frame is fitted and belted in position, the top of the frame should be just level with your ears, with the base snugging into your lower back on a line with the top of the pelvis.

The pelvis is just about where the hip-belt should be located. Remember that it is a hip-belt and *not* a waist-belt and that it should be cinched as tightly as comfortably possible. Properly positioned and secured, this padded band transfers most of the pack weight from shoulders to hips. Get the belt right and adjustment of those shoulder straps (firm enough to prevent pack sway but not overtight so as to affect arm movement) is merely a formality.

With the anatomic unit, the hip-belt is usually worn slightly higher than with the

Internal rigid frame

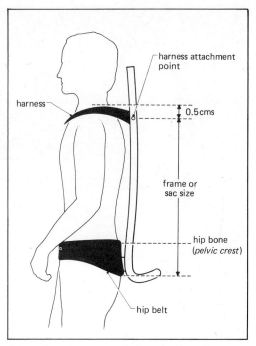

harness attachment point

harness

0.5 cms

frame or sac size

hip bone (*pelvic crest*)

hip belt

Obtaining the correct fit for a backpack

frame pack, though it is still closer to the pelvis than to the waistline. The procedure for putting it on should be the same. Belt up first, then adjust shoulder straps firmly but not overtightly. Look at your profile in the shop mirror now, with the pack trial-loaded.

The image should reflect a smoothly contoured addition to your back, close fitting from hips to shoulders and with reasonable clearance between the back of your head and the top of the pack. It should of course be nicely proportional to your physique, with no tendency to upset your normal stance and balance. This is an important factor later on – perhaps at the end of a strenuous day over rough terrain.

Comfort – or the lack of it – should be felt almost instantaneously, but bear in mind that a new pack, like new hill-walking boots, needs a modicum of breaking-in. On some models, internal framing can be eased by gentle hand pressure to give an even closer body-moulding fit; others will settle themselves eventually under the constant pressure of internal weight and walking action to your personal outline.

If possible allow this to happen naturally, rather than risk straining or fracturing the frame.

Whatever your final choice, the result should be a pack that 'feels right' and is not too big or too small. There should be no obvious pressure points, but remember that it is a new experience for your body and you will feel a strangeness until familiarity conquers.

The more you wear it the sooner your pack will become easy to heft and carry. Do not be overambitious at first. Take a half-hour stroll on level ground to begin with and leave it at that. Next morning you *may* feel a slight tenderness over hip bones and less so around the shoulders. Allow time for this to disappear before repeating the exercise.

Persevere and, though you may think it impossible at first, there will come the magic time (quite often within a week or so) when you can wear your loaded pack for hours on end, almost unaware of its existence. Indeed, you may well join the ranks of those who come to *prefer* walking with a pack, who feel somehow incomplete without it.

Chapter Three
Going to Ground

Stevenson's claim that 'it is better to travel hopefully than to arrive' echoes much of the backpacker's inspiration. We who are hooked on movement for its own sake know that travelling is the real narcotic; final destination is more the concern of package-deal holiday-makers.

We enjoy a different destination *every* night and it is the daily pendulum swing from energetic activity to lair-making for rest and recuperation that makes the game endlessly absorbing and full of variety. No less important, then, than the equipment for mobile efficiency is the camping gear, and the two major items for shelter and slumber are, of course, the tent and the sleeping bag. Since both are of equally vital importance to the wellbeing of the backpacker, they, like the boots and pack, must be considered in some detail.

The tent could be likened to the shell of the snail. It is always with you; because of the limitations on the weight and bulk you can carry, it is fairly confining; it keeps out the rain with great efficiency and the cold some-what less so; and it provides privacy, something that all animals require from time to time.

The question is: which tent? Although it may be very comforting to know that there are so many quality lightweight tents now avail-able, of every shape, size and specification, the choice is a problem none the less. Some very expensive mistakes can be made – not because a given tent is inefficient or badly constructed, but simply because it is not the most appro-priate choice for the particular type of backpacking practised by the novice.

Dome tents have their disadvantages but are roomy and comfortable

One-man lightweight tent, tapering in height and width towards the rear

If, for example, you enjoy the camping spells as much, or even more, than cross-country hiking; if you intend to backpack mainly as a couple, or with children; if your pace is likely to be leisurely and your camping stops lengthy: then quite obviously the tent must be roomy.

Conversely, if you are a lone-wolf walker to whom movement is all, with overnighting viewed as little more than an interruption, then the one-man tent of spartan specification may be the ideal answer. These are at extremes of the spectrum, of course. Further variations can range from a couple of very spacious family tents of which the carrying is shared, to no tent at all, simply a plastic survival bag to keep the sleeping bag protected. For most, though, the well-tried middle way will be chosen, to make both walking and camping equally enjoyable.

For those who enjoy solo travel, mainly in summer, and who are fairly spartan by inclination, the single-skin one-man bivouac may prove ideal. This is a very simple but effective design, squared at the front, supported by two upright poles, tapering to the ground at the rear, and wedge-shaped in profile.

It has a sewn-in groundsheet and zipped entrance flaps which can be press-studded to the porch roof to provide a sheltered cooking area. Advantages are: minimal weight and bulk when packed (around 3 pounds); speed and simplicity of pitching and striking; low initial cost; good aerodynamics in storms, especially when the rear of the tent is faced into any prevailing wind; and good sitting headroom.

These units are favoured by members of the armed services, many youth groups and those who like to spend as much time as possible actually travelling. They are popular with enthusiasts who, for one reason or another, wish to keep pack weight to the absolute minimum.

Disadvantages are: limited internal room for kit storage; no insulation at all against cold; and, whilst the material itself is totally waterproof, a certain amount of damp penetration is inevitable in prolonged rainy spells. If you only want a tent for wind shelter, privacy, protection from summer showers and space saving, this type may well fit the bill.

Of course, you do not have to opt for the wedge shape. There are a number of orthodox single-skin ridge tents in the ultra-lightweight range which are of excellent quality. The Swedes, for instance, have a name in this field. There are also a great number of cheap, mass-produced examples which are not really worthy of serious consideration.

We now come to the main group of backpacking tents, all of which are fully flysheeted. It is this double-skin design which makes them eminently suitable for year-round use. Everyone knows that a flysheet makes the tent totally waterproof; not quite so many are aware that the magic air-space between outer and inner provides efficient insulation and a warmer (or cooler) internal temperature.

The basic ridge design is still top favourite with tent makers and this applies to ultra-lightweight models produced expressly for backpackers, just as much as to larger, heavier units. It is a brilliantly simple design, totally effective and almost impossible to improve upon. It has stood the test of time and is as efficient now as it was a hundred years ago. To shed rain water, remain impervious to storm-force winds and provide maximum snugness, as well as being quick to pitch and strike, the low-profile inverted V-shape is supreme.

Add to this simplicity scaling down, making use of every inch of available space, and using gossamer-thin material in the construction, and the result is a super-light, incredibly compact tent that our camping forefathers could scarcely have dreamed about. Fittingly, for a nation that launched camping as a leisure pursuit in the first place, we in Britain make some of the best backpacking tents available, in every category of weight and economy.

Specification may vary slightly depending on the manufacturer, but will approximate to the following. The one-person unit will provide a sleeping space roughly $6\frac{1}{2}$ feet long, $3\frac{1}{2}$ feet wide at the front and about 3 feet high. Width and height taper at the rear to something like $2\frac{1}{2}$ feet square.

Since the tent is designed basically for sleeping, its entrance is decidedly of the crawl-in type and once settled you cannot move about much. A very cosy shelter, though, within which you can sleep comfortably and brew up or indulge in simple cooking by propping yourself on one elbow. Since most of the time inside will be spent sleeping, the limited space can be tolerated quite happily in summer or for short trips.

The all-important flysheet will be made of rip-stop coated nylon or dacron and will extend right down to ground level at the sides and rear, with an extended frontal porch to provide cooking and kit-storage space. Closure is invariably via a nylon zip with tapes for fastening back.

Securing points will be through short rubber bands and/or D-rings, which enable you to peg the flysheet tautly through the rings, or ease it in windy conditions. Triangular pegs will be of light yet strong alloy, and can be pushed home (in Britain at least), by hand or with the heel of the boot.

The inner tent, usually secured with alloy pin pegs, has a sewn-in tray groundsheet, sometimes but not always of slightly heavier material than the flysheet. A tray groundsheet, as the name implies, is one where the waterproof floor is extended to form shallow walls below the inner tent roof, which will be made of cotton or permeable nylon. A double zip system secures the inner front wall which should be of proofed material (so that fully open it forms a groundsheet for the porch area), and adjustable for ventilation.

It is the 'breathable' inner tent material which so efficiently keeps condensation to a minimum; condensation was a very real problem with early models but happily it is now almost entirely eradicated. Moisture generated by the human body passes through the cotton or permeable nylon inner and settles on the underside of the flysheet. It then drips eventually to the ground from the edges of the flysheet, which are well away from the sleeping camper.

Poles will be either sectional or telescopic and may be two simple uprights (long front, short rear), or a more complex A-pole system, heavier and bulkier, but allowing unimpeded entrance access. This unit can, with practice, be pitched or struck easily within a few minutes; it will weigh around $3\frac{1}{2}$ pounds and will roll up to a package (including pegs but excluding poles), 10 inches by 6 inches, or less.

The two-man ridge is merely a larger version and, since initial cost is not appreciably higher, it must be strongly recommended, *even for solo use.* For living space is appreciably more than in the one-person unit, especially the sitting headroom. Overall length may not be much more, but certainly width and height increase may be as much as a foot – a great deal in tent terms. Only the potential user can decide, though, whether the additional load to be carried (two-man units weigh in at around 5 to $5\frac{1}{2}$ pounds) is worth the luxury of that extra space. Again, this may be vital to one person, immaterial to another.

The manufacture of *ultra*-lightweight tents (as opposed to the fine-quality Egyptian cotton *lightweight* models, which we have long been renowned for making) began in volume production in Britain in the mid-1960s. At this time they were virtually all of basic ridge design.

In the course of evolution a few distinct departures from this tried and trusted shape emerged, and some bold experiments with the new wonder materials were tried. Most were short lived, though one or two have proved winners. Among these is the wedge already described, and especially the more sophisticated version which is fully flysheeted. With this version, the user has the benefit of full sitting headroom at the front end (inner walls being nearly vertical) and unobstructed entrance, since two upright poles are employed to support the squared front end. The flysheet remains basically ridge shaped but with a flattened top panel to match the square-roofed inner. A single short pole supports the rear

end and, from a distance with the tent fully closed, the outline hardly differs from the ridge. That is to say, low, squat and aerodynamic. The drawback is that this model needs to be pitched carefully to achieve good separation between fly and inner. To ensure a good water-shedding profile of the flattened ridge, the tent roof is sloped quite steeply from the front to a point some halfway along the spine. It is here, where it more or less levels out, that there is a danger of the inner and outer touching if pitching is not exact. This is a hazard that the user quickly learns to avoid, but it does mean you have to be fairly meticulous when setting up to prevent a potential leak spot during prolonged wet weather.

The tents thus far listed are amongst the smallest and lightest available and, whilst many are described quite accurately as two-person units, you *do* have to be thin and friendly to use them. They are essentially tents for those who like to keep on the move. The big advantage is that they offer reasonable room for two and luxury space for one.

For those who walk more or less consistently in tandem, the transverse ridge deserves serious consideration. It is yet another brilliant design that evolved originally in Sweden, and is now produced widely by all top tent makers. Outwardly, this unit resembles a ridge tent, albeit of shallow and unusually wide profile, covering something like 11 square feet of usable internal space. And how cunningly this area is utilized. The flysheet is held rigidly in position by two upright poles *and* a ridge pole and the inner tent is positioned across the tent rather than fore and aft. Hence the tent's name. The sleeping comparment layout is very ingenious, for, by making it possible to open both sides with zips, there is access to two spacious areas either side of the bedroom. One area can be used for storage of packs and equipment, the other for cooking and eating.

Top right: *Pitched on a lakeside, a two-man centre-pole ridge tent*
Right: *Traditional two-man centre-pole ridge tent*

They may be opened so that entry access is available from either side and closed independently to cope with any change of wind direction. In this tent the backpacker can hole up in real comfort for prolonged periods, secure in the knowledge that, no matter how foul the elements, occupants will remain snug and dry because of the constant separation of fly and inner provided by ridge pole.

For all but those of the biggest and most robust physique the transverse ridge, weighing in at around $7\frac{1}{2}$ pounds, will almost certainly be considered too heavy for solo work. For two people, however, the problem does not exist. One carries the flysheet and poles; the other the inner tent and pegs. Share-carrying in this manner ensures super-luxury accommodation for a twosome over the most extended trip.

One other model which must be mentioned is the hoop-frame unit. This is igloo-shaped and owes much of its origins to the expedition mountain tent. The most recent arrival to the backpacking range, it is still, in my opinion, in the development stage and models currently available are somewhat complex to pitch and strike. A nylon bubble is supported by tensioned fibreglass rods, and the big selling point is the amount of interior space and overall headroom created by the design. Unfortunately, the tent has numerous rod sections and pitching entails a fiddly system of sleeving and pegging down. Unless you are very patient, pitching, especially in wet or cold conditions, may well be a frustrating procedure. Since it has no weight or bulk advantages over other models, I would not personally recommend this model to the novice.

What then, makes a good tent? Irrespective of the model you do finally select, it should conform to the accepted standard of quality.

Top left: *Another well-made bivouac*
Left: *A tent suitable for year-round use*
Right: *Typical shapes of tent, showing sleeping capacity*

side elevation	ground plan

37

To ensure this you should confine your choice to those models which come from a recognized specialist. This at once eliminates most, if not all, doubts about fitness for purpose, durability and sound investment. Secondly, decide on the type of backpacking you are likely to favour, the maximum weight for your particular physique and, of course, the depth of your pocket.

Having arrived at what you think will be the ideal unit, you must see it pitched before parting with your money. The specialist dealer should arrange this for you and he should be able to help in other ways, particularly if he knows something about your individual requirements.

You should take the tent home and camp on the lawn for a trial spell, preferably with the gear you will normally be carrying. This exercise will usually tell you whether your choice was the right one. If it was not, a reliable retailer will exchange it, provided return is prompt and the tent unmarked. This is a very unlikely contingency if you choose carefully, bearing in mind the points previously mentioned. So, go for a recognized model from an established stable (preferably choosing a tent with a proven track record), and most of the following desirable features should be standard.

The coated nylon flysheet material should be quite soft and supple to the touch – not crackly, or you will have a noisy tent in windy conditions. Crackliness is largely a thing of the past where quality models are concerned, but it is still a point worth checking.

There should not be *too* many nylon cord guylines (although these are sometimes obligatory with larger tents), securing should be mainly by rubber bands so that vigorous shaking to remove heavy dew will not create a bird's nest of tangled guyline.

The porch area should be spacious enough to allow a cooking stove to be positioned *safely* with adequate clearance for both stove and any cooking pot that may be placed on it. Some people prefer a tent where the inner can be struck in foul weather without disturbing the flysheet. This is certainly handy but not absolutely crucial since the whole unit should, anyway, be of a design which can be pitched or struck in minutes, with practice.

Good ventilation is vital and at least one meshed panel should be provided on the inner rear wall. Door panels should zip from the top downwards for additional through venting. Mosquito netting of the inner door is desirable but this can always be added later if necessary.

Unlike cotton tents, nylon units require no 'weathering', except in one small respect. Punch a hole through nylon and it stays the same diameter permanently. There is no subsequent swelling of natural fibre to seal the opening. Quality lightweight-tent makers overcome this little problem very ingeniously by using polyester thread encased in linen. This *does* swell at the first wetting, thus closing the needle holes.

Further proofing is effected by a system of double seaming and the use of dope on all seams to make absolutely sure. Add to this precise shaping of panels and reinforcement patches inserted on all strategic corners, and the result is a unit that is not only functionally first class but has the tailored look which is the hallmark of the quality lightweight. It should also help to illustrate why the good tent is expensive. Those Hong Kong copies may appear superficially identical, but that is where the resemblance ends in nearly all cases. Cheap lightweight tents should be avoided.

A top-class lightweight backpacking tent should, with a modicum of care, give indefinite service and increase your confidence to face even the most severe weather with every outing. You will be appreciating the quality and durability long after you have forgotten the price.

In this chapter we have been discussing the selection of your first tent. As with the backpack, however, it may well be found that there is no ideal all-round tent. Like the small-boat sailor who collects various suits of sails as experience grows and the seasons pass, so the backpacker adds at least one alternative tent to his equipment pile. So, when choosing initially, do not expect the tent to be perfect in every respect. If it fulfils most of your immediate needs, be content. You can always add another thoroughbred to the stable later.

On to the subject of a good night's sleep. At once, it cannot be emphasized too strongly how important this is to the success of every backpacking foray. And generally this means a considerable financial outlay for a quality sleeping bag. Once again, though, the degree of comfort will depend on individuals. What may be acceptable to a nineteen-year-old with an iron constitution might be hopeless for the pampered middle-aged.

The former could be content for example, with a sleeping bag costing no more than £5.00 or so, whilst his older counterpart may well have to pay many times this amount in order to combat the cold night air. Here, then, is a selection to suit most needs and pockets, starting with the cheap, but not necessarily nasty, kapok-filled model.

Produced primarily for scouts, youth groups and hitch-hiking students, this is, with certain reservations, not bad as a summer-weight starter. With a limited life and none too well made in the first place, it has nevertheless two virtues. It is commendably efficient and it rolls small.

Camping on the Devon/Cornwall border

Efficient because kapok is that naturally warm waste-cotton material much favoured by Asiatics for the padding of winter clothing. Generally it is simply quilted and supplied with a short zip and sewn-on cover into which it rolls when packed. The latter may be stuffed with a pullover at night to form an attached pillow. Adequate if finances are slim, but *only* for summer camping at valley level.

Higher up the quality scale from here, there are a whole host of sleeping bags in what may be termed the family camping range. Fully zipped, Terylene filled, very well made, these are efficiently warm, easily washable and durable. You can see hundreds of them, of all filling weights and colours, in any good camping shop. Unfortunately they are useless for our purpose.

It is not so much their weight that excludes them, as their enormous bulk. Not excessive for the average car boot maybe, but almost impossible to fit into a backpack and leave room for anything else. Some manufacturers have tried to produce slim-roll models but the filling has to be so sparse in order to reduce bulk that efficiency is disastrously impaired.

Thus there is a distinct jump in price from the kapok unit to the next model: the genuine

lightweight sleeping bag which is curl-feather filled, cambric covered and tapered to provide a close body fit. The Black's Good Companions comes within this category and several manufacturers make similar models for summer backpacking. These do represent good value for money.

Strongly constructed of tough cambric, there is a drawstring at the top, optional zip for ease of entry and an attached carrying-cover-cum-pillow-case. Weight is about 4 pounds. A slightly superior version in the same range is the Pal-O-Mine which has a mixed feather and down filling. Although this bag looks and feels plumper than the Good Companions it actually weighs less at $3\frac{3}{4}$ pounds and is warmer due to the down content. This is classified as a three-season bag.

Up the price scale again, this time to a very popular spring-through-autumn sleeping bag, the first of the fully down-filled units: the Point Five Orion. This is the type I would urge you to select if funds allow. Similar quality units are made by a number of other manufacturers listed at the end of the book. This sleeping bag is ultra-lightweight, weighing just 2 pounds 1 ounce. And it packs down to a diminutive 14 inch by 6 inch roll. The filling is of finest quality (No. 1), goose down, 16 ounces in all and the quilting is of 'walled' construction. That is to say, instead of stitching straight through from outer to inner lining, both are stitched separately to intermediate taping which in effect forms a wall. This walling (a feature of all better-class bags), is usually slanted to retain the filling better and the result is a complete absence of cold spots. The Orion is designed to fit the body fairly closely to conserve warmth, but there is an oval boxed foot and the shaped hood can be drawn up partially or fully, depending on temperature.

The outer and inner covers are of plain nylon and this quite slippery material enables the user to move around fairly easily inside the bag. There is no access zip. It is available in standard or long size ($82\frac{1}{2}$ inches or 88 inches respectively), and separate stuff-sack is supplied.

At this point a few words about the value of down as a sleeping bag filling may not come amiss. Despite the enormous technological advances with man-made fibres, there is – as yet – nothing to equal the efficiency and sheer cosiness of down. Most of the world's supply comes from China. That it is in very short supply is not surprising when you realize that only about 12 grams can be plucked from the breast of each goose or duck, and the cost of raw down has consequently rocketed in the past few years.

Anatomy of a well-constructed sleeping bag

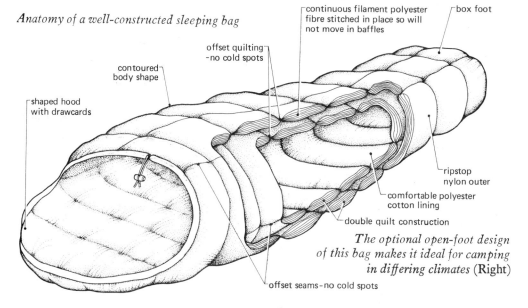

continuous filament polyester fibre stitched in place so will not move in baffles

box foot

offset quilting -no cold spots

contoured body shape

shaped hood with drawcards

ripstop nylon outer

comfortable polyester cotton lining

double quilt construction

The optional open-foot design of this bag makes it ideal for camping in differing climates (Right)

offset seams - no cold spots

Add to this the very complex production technique involved in specialist sleeping-bag manufacture and you begin to see why the retail price is often very much higher than the novice may expect. Goose or duck down has a unique characteristic in that it 'lofts' just like yeast when pressure from compacting is released. It does not form clumps but fluff-balls which retain a high percentage of air, so delicate yet springy is the construction of each particle. It is this down/air mixture that provides warmth without weight.

The human body produces something like 7 ounces of moisture during each night of sleep and this has to be dispersed through breathable covers. And nothing breathes better than the down-filled bag, for the air within is constantly circulating. Thus you stay not only warm but dry, which is equally important when you are spending late autumn or winter nights out of doors.

Whilst it is true that the down-filled bag is superior to all others, it must be admitted that a number of synthetic fillings come pretty close to the real thing, especially Dacron Hollofil. This is a polyester product consisting of short lengths of freely moving fibres, coated to reduce friction. A permanent crimp to give that essential springiness is given mechanically to the fibre. This scores over orthodox solid polyester strands since, microscopically, it

appears more like macaroni than spaghetti. This reduces fibre weight and at the same time gives a small but significant improvement in the warmth-to-weight ratio. It also improves compressibility.

What then does this mean in layman's terms? Simply that it is now possible to produce a sleeping bag that is *nearly* as good as the down version and which can be compressed to *almost* the same packed size. Whilst it is very difficult to make accurate comparisons between fillings, you could say that a given weight of Hollofil is roughly equivalent to the same weight of a fairly good down-and-feather mix.

Three big advantages of the polyester-filled sleeping bag. It is not quite so expensive initially; it is highly resistant to water so that insulation is almost unaffected in wet conditions; and it can be machine washed like any other synthetic material. I must say that, so far as duvet coats and waistcoats are concerned, I find the synthetic filling actually superior to down in all but true arctic conditions. For sleeping though, especially in a quality light-weight tent which remains as dry as the proverbial bone, I prefer to be surrounded by goose down.

Full four-season sleeping bags will only be briefly touched upon here, since few novices opt for the high-cost super-luxury models

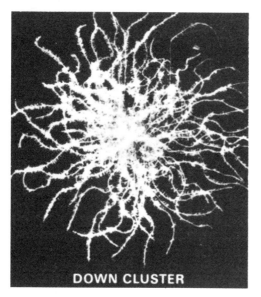

DOWN CLUSTER

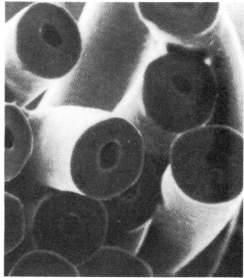

initially. These are invariably barrel shaped, often double layered with bag-within-a-bag construction and tailored mummy hoods. Something like double the volume of down used in the Orion comprises the filling, or maybe a down and curl-feather mix since the latter retains its loft somewhat longer. The theory is that the slightly coarser feathers help to retain separation of the gossamer-like down particles.

Weight and bulk is of course considerably higher than the three-season variety. I might just add that ownership of a such a deluxe unit is not obligatory for winter backpacking in the temperate zone, as you will see in due course. Within this luxury range by the way, you can buy bags with left and right full zips, so that two units can be joined for sleeping double.

Whatever your final choice of sleeping bag, it pays dividends to treat it with respect. Never leave the bag tightly rolled between trips, especially the down-filled variety. Hang full-length if possible, in an airy cupboard to keep the filling sweet and retain maximum loft. One of the special sleeping-bag hangers that retailers use for display is ideal.

Fibre-filled sleeping bags are easily washable, although this should be an occasional rather than a regular treatment, for over-

Above: (Left) *magnified speck of down compared with* (right), *the efficient but not quite so warm man-made Hollofil*
Right: *How the Karrimat sleeping insulator works*

washing will gradually reduce the 'body' of the filling. With the down-filled bag washing should really be avoided altogether. Far better grubby and efficient than clean and useless. It is only your dirt anyway.

If you must wash any down-filled bag, do it in the bath, using tepid water and one of the special preparations like Soppi, a Dutch product which will not remove the natural oils from the down. Rinse in copious changes of cold water and tease the down periodically but thoroughly during drying. This is a long and tedious process and should only be undertaken as a last resort.

Far better to prevent soiling by using a sheet liner, even though this means a modest addition to pack bulk and weight. Liners are available as singles, doubles, in cotton or nylon, barrel shaped or rectangular. They are usually taped at the foot for tying securely into the sleeping bag itself and slit with more tie-tapes at the top for easy access. A pillow cover completes the specification. Easily made up

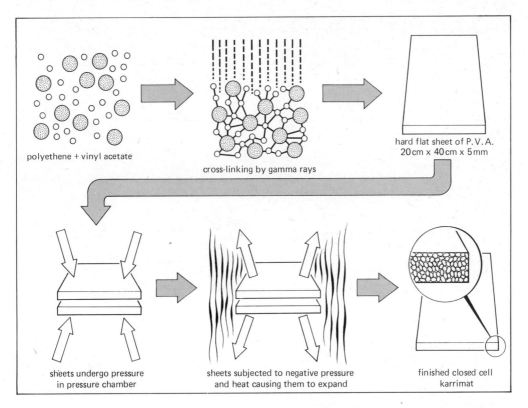

polyethene + vinyl acetate

cross-linking by gamma rays

hard flat sheet of P.V.A.
20cm x 40cm x 5mm

sheets undergo pressure
in pressure chamber

sheets subjected to negative pressure
and heat causing them to expand

finished closed cell
karrimat

at home from spare sheeting if funds are limited.

There is one other item necessary to ensure the sleeping bag always operates at full efficiency, namely a sleeping mat. And I simply cannot stress too strongly how crucial is this modest and quite cheap piece of back-packing equipment. How we ever camped at all before its invention is now difficult to comprehend. A whole variety of these is now available, though the original and still, I think, the best is that manufactured by Karrimor and sold under the brand name Karrimat. So good is the product in fact that the name has become almost generic amongst outdoor-life enthusiasts. Simply, it is a closed-cell foam mat some 10 millimetres thick, light as a feather, exceedingly tough, long-lasting and totally waterproof and with such a sheet underneath your sleeping bag you could sleep warm on glacier ice.

No matter how expensive or well filled the sleeping bag, where your body compresses the filling against the earth, there is bound to be a serious heat loss. The Karrimat prevents this in the most dramatic and effective manner. As vital to the camper's comfort as the sleeping bag itself, the Karrimat will not do *very* much to soften your sleeping patch, though it does take off that iron hardness. What it will guarantee, though, is night-long and complete protection against cold, whatever the ground temperature.

It has two other important assets: it can be laid under the tent groundsheet to protect the latter against damage on flinty terrain; and it will serve as a useful sit-mat during daytime rest breaks. It comes in standard, short, or king-sized rolls, or it can be bought by the metre, 3 millimetres thick. This thinner version is not quite so robust, but is popular with those who like to keep pack bulk to the minimum. Insulation is still absolute and some backpackers use shaped lengths of 3 milli-metres to make up a full floor covering for the tent.

Chapter Four
Auxiliary Equipment

By this stage you should have progressed from complete novice to the class of 4B : Boots, Backpack, Bivouac, Bedding. There is one more subject to be taken, however, before technical graduation to those beckoning hills. And this concerns the backpacking auxiliary gear.

Collectively these items ensure that you remain efficiently fed, watered and immune to the elements, whether tramping or tenting, and comfortable through daylight and darkness. The most important of these is the cooking stove.

This is not merely a device to brew tea or sizzle bacon, but could in an emergency become a life-saver. You will probably never use it to combat hypothermia while benighted on some mountain in white-out conditions. Just in case, though, go for quality and fitness for purpose when choosing.

There was a time, of course, not so many years ago, when the prime cooking and heating source of the lightweight camper was the wood fire. Even during the 1950s the Forestry Commission were not only permitting, but urging, tenters to burn all the dead wood they could find in the New Forest, for example, on their camp fires.

This seems almost incredible now and, unless you intend packing in Africa or the Outback, the friendly camp fire, regrettably, will be a rare enjoyment in your backpacking career. That's progress though, and we can do little more than conform in the main if we wish to stay legal and do our bit towards preserving the ecology.

Happily, there are now some excellent stoves available, designed expressly for backpackers. Here are some that have proven their

Camping with an early style tent

A windshield aids the preparation of supper

worth to our fraternity which I will list by the fuels used to power them.

Butane liquid-gas units are almost exclusively favoured by contemporary family campers. The big advantages are simplicity of operation, cleanliness and speedy efficiency. There is a variety of miniaturized versions for enthusiasts carrying lightweight equipment; some of these operate from almost any type of available cannister, through flexible piping and/or alternative connectors.

Whilst the burner unit itself may be miniscule, assembly and dismantling are sometimes fiddly and, if standard-sized throwaway gas cartridges are used, pack bulk is a consideration.

One of the best units, in my opinion, is the Camping Gaz Globetrotter, in which both burner and cartridge are about as small as is practically possible. What is more, the alloy two-part casing converts into $\frac{1}{2}$ litre saucepans. The stove travels fully assembled and ready

for instant use, and the tiny, slimline gas cannisters can be stored away in odd corners of the pack.

The Globetrotter boils a saucepan full of water in about $4\frac{1}{2}$ minutes in windless conditions, it sits nice and low on the ground (an important consideration under a pup tent flysheet), and the foldaway pot platform is shaped to prevent saucepan slide. I have used one of these for three years now and it is still in perfect working order. It weighs 1 pound and is supplemented by a 7 inch diameter, coated frying pan with a folding handle. It satisfies all cooking needs for solo *summertime* trips.

The disadvantages are: high running costs; limited burning life of the cartridges (about $1\frac{3}{4}$ hours continuous use); and unsuitability of the unit for cold-weather or high-altitude conditions. When the mercury drops, gas pressure is seriously affected, particularly with partially full cartridges, so this stove is not recommended outside the May/September period in Great Britain.

This stove is about 8 inches high, the saucepan 4 inches across

That old favourite, the paraffin-burning Primus, is nowadays enjoying something of a renaissance, thanks to the enormous growth of lightweight camping and travel. A stove for all seasons this, beautifully made of gleaming brass, traditional and trustworthy through many decades.

Virtues of this Swedish old-timer are: high efficiency; very economical running; universal availability of fuel; and a flame that can be adjusted from the gentlest glimmer to the ferocity of a blow-torch. Of robust construction, it is easy to service and maintain and spares kits are available everywhere.

Drawbacks are: initial high cost; somewhat complex stove assembly and priming ritual, which entails carrying separate starter liquid or paste; and a heavy weight (just under 2 pounds) due to the brass content.

It hardly seems fair to award penalty points because assembly and priming is somewhat long-winded. On many occasions time is not of the essence; there are, though, moments when you want ignition quickly and with as little fuss as possible. Unless you are always patient, the meths-burning Trangia may well prove more attractive in the early stages, if not permanently.

This Swedish cooker is unquestionably top favourite with backpackers. It is not so much a stove as a complete cooking system with saucepans, frying pan and even an optional extra mini-kettle. All aluminium, except for the brass burner unit, high quality, heavy duty and superbly turned, the component parts nestle – Russian-doll fashion – within each other, to form a neat and compact travel set. Weight of the one-man version is approximately $1\frac{3}{4}$ pounds.

The domed wide-bottomed base is ingeniously designed and very stable. The cooker has a low profile with a totally enclosed flame – making it very safe. Assembly and ignition is a commendably brief business. A big feature of the Trangia is the way it actually

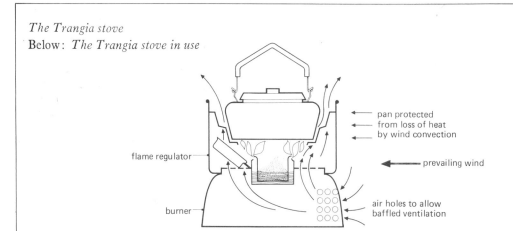

The Trangia stove
Below: *The Trangia stove in use*

flame regulator

burner

pan protected
from loss of heat
by wind convection

◀── prevailing wind

air holes to allow
baffled ventilation

thrives on draughts. The harder the wind blows the quicker it boils water.

No other camping stove has so many advantages. Add to this the absence of jets to clog, and priming mechanism to jam or wear out, and you begin to understand why the stove is so popular. Simply assemble, pour in a modest amount of meths (about two dessert spoonsful for a brew) and within four minutes or so the tea's made.

The standard one-man version consists of a saucepan, a frying pan which doubles as the saucepan lid, and a pot handle liberally holed to dissipate heat and keep down weight. The burner has an interior wick which effectively produces a gas-type flame after a short warm-up period. There is a flip-over simmer ring, and a second aid to regulating is provided by the base which has a series of air holes on one side and is blanked on the other. The space around the burner when the unit is packed can be used for tea bags, sugar and dried milk in small amounts. Thus the tea-making kit is self contained, unless you opt for the extra kettle, which takes up this dry-goods space. The two-man Trangia is simply a larger version with two saucepans and a larger optional kettle.

Methylated spirit is readily available at most hardware shops or chemists, but if you intend travelling well away from the beaten track a reserve of fuel will be needed. Practice will tell you how much. Meths is a safe fuel since, like paraffin, it has a low flash point. It is also clean and virtually non-toxic. However, it does 'creep' easily, so a really leakproof fuel container is obligatory. The Sigg bottle is first favourite – aluminium with a deep screw cap. The 1 litre size is probably best since the Trangia is not amongst the most economical burners.

Other minor drawbacks are the difficulty of setting a really low flame during prolonged cooking sessions and the greasy soot deposits which do collect on the utensils rather quickly, depending on the spirit quality. If you keep the cuisine simple and do not mind scouring the pans now and then, the Trangia must be number one cooking choice. When you have finished cooking, always allow it to burn out

if you are travelling on. Otherwise, everything in your pack will be permeated with that strong smell. Never attempt to clamp the screw top back into position. This will quickly melt the neoprene sealing ring which in turn will block the tiny flame holes.

This is by no means the extent of cooking-stove choice, there are also some first-class petrol stoves and solid-fuel units which employ meta tablets. The first are primarily favoured by motorcycle campers (who have fuel on tap), the second by day walkers for tea or coffee making; general application is somewhat limited. Both have their supporters in the world of backpacking; solid-fuel units are favoured by those who like to travel really light, living on next to nothing.

Unless you go for the Trangia, a canteen set will be needed. There is a wide choice of the nesting type available – some are practical, others not. Avoid the very cheap, thinly spun variety, which have the nasty habit of producing instant-stick food and are difficult to clean. Basic kits provide a main shallow saucepan, a lid, again doubling as a frying pan, separate or fold-in handles and possibly one or two extra alloy plates.

In practice, you may well find it better to build your own cuisine kit. Much depends whether you are into Ying and Yang or are one of the bangers-and-mash brigade. Certainly the Teflon-coated folding frying pan is recommended. The 7 inch diameter model is easy to pack, easy to cook on, doubles as a plate and, importantly, can be cleaned with a minimum of water – always precious when you have to carry it. With this, plus a canteen of decent capacity (in case you have to cook a lot of freeze-dried foods), you can cope perfectly well.

The knife-fork-spoon sets, lightweight and compact, are popular, though some prefer a heavy-duty sheath or jack-knife, and a spoon and fork from the kitchen drawer. Multi-purpose gadget knives are exotic but expensive and seldom fully utilized. They are also bulky and a bit fiddly. If you buy a sheath-knife, make sure the blade is the legal 6 inch length and is robust enough to chop as well as slice. If the jack-knife is preferred, go for something simple but strong with a really strong rivet where it folds into the handle. Gun shops often carry superb examples of both, notably Scandinavian or German.

Since your drinking vessel is likely to prove important (for there is nothing like backpacking to work up a thirst), a word or two about choice. The old-fashioned enamel mug is tough, but it does chip easily and you need iron lips to drink hot tea from it. One asset is that you can pop it back on top of the stove *briefly* if the drink cools too quickly.

Bendable plastic mugs pack well, are cheap enough to be expendable and lightweight. Nowadays they are relatively taint-free. My favourite kind of mug, however, is the Insulex double-skin design of rigid plastic which keeps hot drinks effectively hot longer than any other kind, which is a real advantage in the outdoors. It stains fairly quickly but can be cleaned with Melfresh or even tooth powder. Do not scour or you will quickly remove the glaze.

Separate plates and eating bowls are something of a luxury when backpacking, since the frying pan and canteen can perfectly well double as plates, but some people prefer them. The bendable plastic soup plate (deep enough to prevent food sliding off) and cereal bowls are quite popular and they do pack easily and weigh little.

Salt and pepper is a must for most but, if you choose one of the combined cellars, make sure it has a really air-tight top and cannot be spilled. Many old hands prefer to use pill bottles or those small metal tablet containers with positive screw tops.

A screw top will be necessary too on any plastic jar used for carrying butter or margarine. Snap tops come adrift easily and the result inside your pack if this happens could be ruinous to any down-filled sleeping bag, not to mention clothing. If you like cooking oil, then use a screw-top bottle and make doubly sure by sheathing it with a plastic bag.

Dry goods are best carried in plastic bags, again doubled if in doubt, to keep weight and bulk to the minimum. A mini-sized tin opener takes up no room. If you are a non-smoker, do not forget matches or a lighter, and always keep the former protected from damp, both in camp and when under way.

So to the all-important water supply. The standard twosome with most backpackers is a personal water bottle of $\frac{1}{2}$ or 1 litre capacity, depending on need for en-route drinks, plus a folding water bag with tap for base-camp use. The first may be a simple plastic bottle (again with a foolproof stopper *and* screw cap), which is cheap and quite adequate.

Or, at the top end of the scale, there are those beautifully made French alloy flasks internally coated with enamel so that water (or wine) remains untainted. These kidney-shaped containers have simple but positive snap-down stoppers and dog clips for fastening to belt or outside of pack. They also help to keep water cool, but they are somewhat expensive. In between there are many alternatives from British Army style to blanket-swathed American frontier canteens. With any lower priced metal bottle check the seams and the stopper with a trial fill in the shop before paying your money.

The roll-up water carrier provides a really generous $2\frac{1}{2}$ gallons on tap in camp, yet is merely a slim roll of tough, non-toxic plastic with wooden dowel strengtheners in transit. It tucks away unobtrusively in the pack, is very strongly made and has an excellent non-drip tap. It can be hung from a tree or simply laid on the ground.

Like the Karrimat, this really is an essential item to the backpacker. Reasonably priced and long lasting, the carrier discolours internally quite quickly, but this in no way affects the quality of the drinking water. The bag has an ingenious combined tap and push-in bung, held simply by plastic serrations. It works perfectly, with one proviso. Do not carry it filled with the tap facing your leg. An inadvertent knock when walking over rough ground will make the bung pop out, and you get an instant bootful. No joke on a cold and frosty morning.

Top right: *A selection of available light-camping gear*
Right: *A selection of useful, lightweight cooking gear and food*

Candle lantern

Light during high summer hardly poses a problem for the backpacker, since it rarely becomes inky black. However, artificial light is needed in winter and sometimes early or late in the season. An ordinary scout torch or even one of those diminutive pen-lights will be sufficient in July, since it will rarely, if ever, come out of the pack.

Any other times of year something more substantial is required. One of the best lamps available to the lightweight camper is the French Wonderlamp. This is a flat torch powered by a $4\frac{1}{2}$ volt battery, with a plug-in headlamp extension which is worn miner-fashion.

Anyone who has ever tried to prepare a camp meal by the light of an ordinary torch will know what a frustrating business it can be. No matter how you position the thing the beam never seems to shine exactly where you want it. With the Wonderlamp, which is well named, you have this personal headlamp complete with up and down tilt adjustment, always shining precisely in front of you, leaving hands free to get on with the work.

The extension lead is long enough for the unit to be hung conveniently from the top of the tent, and the torch itself may be used independently. The battery will give sufficient light for two nights of winter backpacking if used intelligently, and the flat batteries are common enough to be stocked by every village store.

Some enthusiasts like to supplement this working light with one of the long-life sterine candles inside the tent. No need to warn you about the dangers here, though they are safe if used with care. Always gouge out a hole to take at least an inch of the candle base in the porch area and ensure there is adequate head-room between flame and flysheet roof. To make the candle last even longer, fashion a wax catcher from foil, so that it burns like a nightlight.

Candlelight is romantic but very limited, though it does make for a cosy in-tent environment and you do get a mini heat source as a bonus. A welcome extra illumination then, especially on a wild or cold night, but do make sure it is safe. There are candle lanterns available, even lightweight telescopic ones, but they smoke up somewhat and are often messy to operate with a habit of scattering molten wax about.

Of course, there is nothing to prevent you enjoying the illumination of a gas lantern if you are prepared to carry it. Some think it worthwhile, but you do pay a daytime penalty of weight and bulk, which over a longish distance may prove to be unacceptable. As stated though, the lantern has its fans, especially for deep winter camping, for it does give a bright light and quite an appreciable amount of warmth. An undoubted comfort when some fourteen hours or so out of every twenty-four are dark. If you opt for a lantern make sure you have a few spare mantles, for they are extremely fragile once burned off.

Whilst on the subject of bleaker elements, let's consider the question of personal protection. Not so much against cold, which I want to deal with at some length later, but the more frequent hazards of Britain's basically temperate climate : wind and rain.

There really is nothing more miserable than being wet through at the end of a day's trek, with the prospect of long hours of incarceration in a damp tent ahead and no chance of drying out. The spirits of even the staunchest can plummet in such circumstances, and more than one novice thus caught out has given up the game there and then. This is his, or her, loss; for properly kitted-out backpacking in the rain (whilst never wonderfully enjoyable), can be a kind of masochistic fun when you *know* you will stay dry and warm beneath the outer garments. This blissful state can only be achieved with a quality rain suit, and again these do not come cheaply.

Mention wet-weather gear and you at once enter another area of backpacking controversy. Everyone seems to have their own view of what constitutes the ideal. Certainly the over-garments must be multi-functional and, to help you make up your own mind, I indicate below what qualities they should possess.

Obviously they must be waterproof, but they should also be windproof (to retain body heat at higher altitudes), cut generously to keep the bogey of condensation to a minimum, and yet be lightweight and compact so they do not take up too much precious pack space.

This is asking a lot. You can, for instance, stay totally dry in an oilskin suit and this is fine if you are on a boat. But it would be ludicrous to carry such a heavy, bulky combination on a cross-country hike. At the other extreme, you could buy a thin nylon anorak weighing almost nothing which packs into its own breast pocket and can be clipped, like an outsize goitre to the waist for dry-weather walking. Passable for brief, high-summer showers maybe, but you are likely to find more moisture by way of condensation under the garment than that falling from the heavens. A compromise is probably the best, and within this category the G & H Cagjac has a first-class reputation – pleasing, for it is made in Yorkshire, where they know about bad weather.

The Cagjac, awarded a Gear of the Year Award by *Climber and Rambler* magazine, is made from a *substantial* nylon material which, though *fairly* lightweight, and acceptably compact, is none the less stout enough to stand up to long-term strap abrasion and the general rough and tumble of outdoor life. It gives excellent protection against the heaviest and most prolonged rain and condensation is

Overtrousers such as these, with a zip fastener at the ankle, can be extremely useful. Boots need not be removed as overtrousers are shed

reduced to a level where it can be virtually ignored.

Proofing is provided by multi-coat polyurethane spraying inside and all the seams are specially treated. The Cagjac is approximately knee length with a heavy-duty two-way nylon zip, itself protected by a Velcro-fastened flap. This not only keeps out the wet but ensures that the garment is totally windproof too. Inner cuffs are elasticated (and adjustable), spacious pockets are specially sewn to prevent water entry, the collar is really stormproof and the hood generous and drawcorded for foul weather conditions.

No less vital than the rain top, are the overtrousers. Though some do try to cope without, they will be needed sooner rather than later. For, no matter how voluminous a raincoat you have, in any persistent downpour, trousers and socks will soon be soaked through. Good backpacking overtrousers are easy to slip on or off, without removing boots, being fitted with long side zips and elasticated waistbands.

There are other brand-name suits of similar specification and quality. Berghaus is one recommended. Their Thor Suit jacket is of slightly shorter length than the Cagjac, but it

has a wire-stiffened hood peak, a feature much appreciated by some spectacle wearers. Various colours are available with both suits, from safety orange to mud green for those who like to blend with the background. Whatever your final choice, do make sure it is generous enough to be worn *comfortably* with extra pullovers beneath.

Lighter weight nylon anoraks and over-trousers are preferred by some enthusiasts, notably those spartans who insist on keeping pack size small. And the Cagoulle (French for cape) is another favourite in this category. Originally produced for climbers, it is long enough to cover your knees when in the sitting position.

Better quality models, like those made by Blacks of Greenock, are good rain-shedders and they do keep the wind out, but they are prone to condensation, especially when the walking gets strenuous. These are donned by pulling over the head; they usually have a short zip at the neck and a breast pocket which should be large enough to take a standard Ordnance Survey map.

Three more possibilities, just to illustrate the variety available, are the Pacjac, Gore-Tex Rainwear and the Belstaff waxed jacket. The first would hardly merit a *Tailor and Cutter* fashion award, but it is very practical, enveloping the whole walker from head to foot, backpack included. Weighing only 11 ounces, and made from polyurethane-coated nylon, this sleeveless, hooded poncho is a kind of mobile storm shelter, allowing good freedom of movement and air circulation to keep down condensation. You may look a bit like Quasimodo, but this hardly matters when it is raining stair rods.

Gore-Tex, a newish material now familiar to many backpackers, is an American product invented by W. L. Gore. It has made a significant development to the manufacture of waterproof clothing. It is not so far the automatic choice for rainwear and a mass breakthrough to the popular market has yet to happen. Not least because of price, which is significantly higher than for comparable materials.

Briefly, Gore-Tex is a micro-porous film which is laminated between fabric layers. This film, with no less than nine billion pores per square inch, allows vapour to pass freely but no liquid, and is thus condensation free.

Discoloration, seaming and the 'feel' were early problems, but there is no doubt that the material has a lot going for it in the future. Currently the Berghaus range of Gore-Tex garments have largely conquered the snags, but the price is still, for many, prohibitive.

The Belstaff waxed-cotton jacket would be my recommendation to those who like natural material. This model, approved by Chris Bonnington incidentally, is totally waterproof, acceptably lightweight and rolls up very small. Tough and traditionally well made by another British firm, it is unlined and relies simply on the waxed coating to keep out water. This it does staunchly and for a prolonged period. When it does finally dry out, you simply apply another coat of the proprietary wax. One drawback, it does feel 'tacky' and will grease-mark anything absorbent, particularly when new. Frankly, so functional is the Belstaff that this is a hazard worth accepting.

This more or less completes the *basic* backpacking outfit and, I hope, the major part of the financial outlay. There are a number of other items which will be considered as we progress, most of which can be collected piecemeal as needs dictate and funds allow. Right now it is time to gather up the bits and pieces and put them to the use for which they are intended. So let's get on the path.

A good-quality cagoule is an essential item

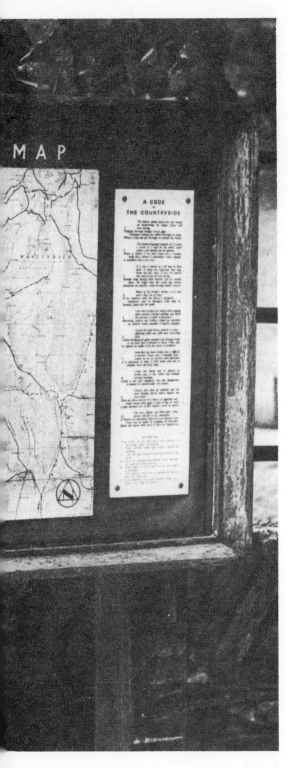

Detailed footpath maps are quite common in
popular walking areas

Chapter Five
Best Foot Forward

It will pay long-term dividends to make sure
the maiden voyage is a successful one –
especially if your everyday life is largely spent
cocooned against the elements. Temper
enthusiasm with caution, and choose carefully
the time and place for that very important first
excursion.

Late spring or early summer is ideal; but
do not be too rigid with your plans. You may,
for example, have a weekend (the first expedition should not really be of more than two
or three nights' duration) set aside, but if this
happens to fall in the middle of depressing
weather postpone it until conditions improve.

You will have plenty of time to pit yourself
against the elements, but wait until experience
and familiarity with equipment make light of
any adverse conditions. Such forethought is
particularly necessary if you want to convert
any other member of the family who may not
yet *quite* share your own enthusiasm.

Only you know whether your inclination is
to walk alone or with others. Husband and
wife teams form a fair proportion of the backpacking fraternity and there is a sprinkling of
family walkers too, often accompanied by
quite small children. By far the biggest
percentage, however, go it alone. If you walk
in company, you had better choose your co-
walkers carefully to make sure you are
compatible, particularly when it comes to
daily mileages, walking pace, feeding and
drinking habits and so on.

The typical backpacker is a bit of a loner,
albeit a friendly one, with a natural yearning
to escape periodically all ties. Indeed, much of
the satisfaction of the game comes from being
a perambulatory ship in the night, so that

Youth hostels are useful, but seldom necessary when conditions are this fine

friendly contact can be casually made, or not, as mood dictates, and terminated at will.

Here you are, then, on the appointed day. With any luck, the sun is shining and your objective is a stretch of fairly gentle English footpath. Possibly a low-level route through Dovedale, part of the South Downs Way, or a coastal path almost anywhere around scenic Britain. There are two reasons for suggesting these examples.

Firstly you will not have trouble tracing your route, for the path will be well defined; there will be no need to indulge in a lot of map and compass work (though of course you must have both aids with you), and you will never be uncomfortably far from village shops, pubs or public transport. Or your own car if, for any reason, you have to abort the outing.

Let's start the final preparations, then, with personal clothing. Time was when the traditional sailcloth anorak was automatic choice for the walker. Some still favour this service-able windproof garment. Many more now make their wet-weather jacket serve as wind-cheater when necessary, relying on pullovers for comfort and warmth most of the time, supplemented by shirt and undervest if preferred.

Make sure that pullovers have a fair percentage of natural wool content and remember that two thin ones give better insulation than one thick. The oiled-wool, fisherman type is very popular as a final top layer since it gives freedom of movement through stretch, clings nicely to pack straps and will take quite a bit of moisture from light rain or mist before it actually becomes wet.

Denim is about the worst material you could choose for hill-country wear. Despite toughness, it does nothing to insulate against cold or wet. Yet hordes of jean-clad walkers seem to manage well enough, at least in summer. Start as you mean to go on, though, and buy a pair of serge or worsted slacks, or at least a pair with a reasonable wool content. Derby tweed backpacking trousers are available, as are breeches, but these are expensive and not

Even on so-called open paths there are 'restrictions' such as these

vital for the gentle trip in mind here.

Before donning your boots for the first time in earnest, it might pay to apply a layer of barrier cream (not foot powder which can be abrasive) to the soles of your feet. Or you can use a smear of the backpacker's friend, Hirstalg. This is an Austrian-made, push-up dispenser of deer fat which really does prevent blisters. Remember it is a prophylactic and will do nothing to relieve soreness once blisters have formed.

Now for the pack, and we will start by emphasizing the importance of the checklist which every backpacker worth his salt refers to, no matter how experienced. It may seem a bit superfluous at this stage, with all that newly acquired gear spread around you on the floor, but if you do not list the gear, sooner or later you will forget something vital.

There is nothing more depressing than to discover some desperate omission miles from anywhere. So write down a list of *every* item

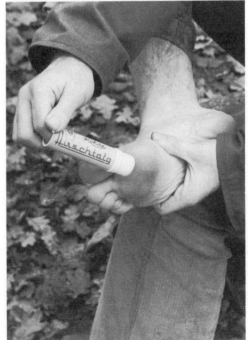

Deer fat is the best way of preventing blisters

you are taking and tick it off physically as you pack. The acknowledged routine for filling a modern high pack is to stow lightweight items at the bottom, heavier bulkier gear at the top and closest to your back to gain the most efficient weight distribution.

Do not be too slavish about this, though, for it is also prudent to pack items needed last furthest from the opening. I personally start with the tent and, no matter what model, I find it pays to remove it from the carrying valise. Two small rolls (the inner and flysheet) and the bag of pegs pack neater than one bundle, and solid objects like torch and so forth travel better sandwiched between the softer material.

Poles are slipped into the appropriate slots which all good packs have inside; they are *never* carried strapped to the outside where they can easily be lost. A couple of plastic bags protect against damp if the tent has to be packed wet.

Karrimat comes next. In summer, I use a short length of 3 millimetre thickness which folds small, and it is positioned so that I can draw it out easily for rest stops during the day. Next the sleeping bag, and once again it is better removed from the stuff sack (which makes a useful shopping bag) and fed into the pack, foot first to prevent air traps, thus forming a nest for hardware like the stove, eating irons, water bag and mug. A spare, thinnish pullover and the ever-ready rain suit tops off the main compartment.

All these items, except the last of course, and the tent poles are stowed in a stout plastic bag before going into the pack. For, no matter how well made, no back pack can be totally waterproof. In any prolonged downpour a small degree of seepage through the seams and access flaps is inevitable. Plastic bag liners ensure tinder dryness whatever the weather.

Side pockets, base compartments or top-flap pocket usually house items like food, fuel and water bottles, toilet kit and optional personal possessions like camera or binoculars, padded perhaps with spare socks or those ever-useful J-cloths.

With any straight-through pack, without pockets, you just have to load all the bits and pieces on top. Some owners use sleeping bag and tent valises or plastic bags to separate items. In the interest of efficiency, it is a good idea to have a place for everything and everything in its place – hence the greater popularity of the compartmented pack. Especially outside the summer season, when the contents will of necessity be increased. Much depends on how casual or tidy minded you are though. So long as you have some kind of system which works for you, it really is immaterial how you achieve it.

For this first trip at least, I would suggest that you do not try to achieve total independence with the food supply. Overloading the pack is neither sensible nor necessary. By all means take tea or coffee ingredients, a chocolate bar, packet of biscuits, perhaps a muesli mix, a small loaf, chunk of cheese, and a small jar of butter or margarine.

For the rest, buy as you go at village stores and do your shopping late in the day to avoid needless humping. Plenty of time later, as experience grows, to discover what your potential pack larder should contain. In any case, as we all know, the idea that you will drop from exhaustion if you do not eat every few hours is a total fallacy.

Indeed, it is positively beneficial to be abstemious. Heavy meals should never be taken during a walking day. Save your appetite for the evening. Anyone in normally healthy condition should be able to manage comfortably on a breakfast, midday snack and main meal late in the day.

Liquid intake is a different matter, and will almost certainly have to be increased as a result of the healthy exertion of walking with a pack. This is no problem if you carry a personal water bottle and/or time your rest spells to coincide with pub hours. So watch the pack loading and remember that every surplus ounce will feel progressively heavier as the day goes on. The backpacker's best friend is a full wallet. Why hump supplies from home if you can buy them when needed?

Getting to the selected trail head by public transport leaves you fancy free but it is seldom as quick or convenient as driving there. Since the majority of backpackers are also car

In widely walked areas like the Lake District backpackers can encounter discouraging notices such as this

owners, the latter is the most popular method. One snag is finding a long-term car park, but this seldom poses too many problems. There may be a car park adjacent to the start, especially if it is a scenic and well-used route. Security here may be doubtful, though, and this practice is only advocated if your car is a banger or you just do not care. Local garages on the other hand are often a good bet (particularly if you fill up as you chat up), pubs equally so.

Other alternatives are locals with garden space (if you have the nerve to ask and offer a fee), cafés with generous parking space or farms. For added peace of mind you can always notify the village police station or house. Not a bad place to inquire anyway if you have trouble parking.

If your destination is distant, it may pay to use a camping site, spend the first night there then set off in the morning. The site owner will usually find you a corner for the car at a modest extra fee. Most of us leave our vehicles with a slight uneasiness at first, but get used to it, and so long as you are insured you soon become philosophical. Lock, leave and forget (tucking the car keys away safely), and concentrate on the footwork.

You will, of course, have a compass and the appropriate Ordnance Survey maps (absolutely essential no matter how well defined the path), which you will quickly discover are your constant reference guides. These cartographic marvels are no mere maps; they are more the portals of discovery. So check your first objective, maybe a scenic high-spot, hamlet or isolated pub, heft your pack and set off.

This is always a marvellous moment. If you have done your homework properly, clothing, pack and boots should be comfortably familiar and there should be an excited anticipatory spring in your step. And why not? Ahead, a sweep of visually stimulating countryside, bisected with that beckoning ribbon of footpath and you – possibly for the first time in years – with nothing more mentally taxing to consider than when you will stop for that first brew-up or glass of beer. If the sun is shining and the birds singing, it is sheer magic.

After a mile or two you may well have to strip off a pullover or two. Again, perhaps for the first time for years, your body is beginning to function as it should, warming up nicely, opening up the pores and ridding itself of toxins. You are not only enjoying yourself; you are on a health kick as well.

As with any sustained physical activity, the sweat comes freely at first then settles to an acceptable level. So do not be too drastic with the pullover peeling. Experience will quickly dictate the right combination of wool layers.

And, talking of experience, do not set yourself too ambitious a target first time out. That old adage about backpacking being not so much miles covered as hours enjoyed is a good one to remember. Particularly when you find yourself speeding up the pace for no apparent reason.

Remember that livestock have an important claim on the land. The country code is for their protection

There is no set rule, of course. Some like to maintain a brisk, unbroken pace between objectives, irrespective of terrain, weather or personal comfort. Others prefer to dawdle along, communing with nature, stopping to stare, or just stopping. No matter, each gains his particular kind of reward. But it does emphasize why you have to choose any walking partner carefully and why so many backpackers prefer going solo.

When you do take a deliberate rest spell, remove your pack, replace that pullover to prevent chilling and, if needs be, loosen or take off your boots. Stretch out full length if possible – here is where the Karrimat may get its first airing – and prop your feet on the pack, if possible slightly higher than your head. Do not stop too long – ten to fifteen minutes is about average – or your muscles will cool off too much and you will find resuming an effort.

A typical backpacking morning may start at around 9.00 a.m. with a short rest at 10.00 a.m. and a longer brew-up break around 11.00 a.m. Another five minutes at midday and then a picnic or pub lunch around 1.00 p.m. This should be leisurely and protracted; it may last a couple of hours and there is no reason why you should not indulge in a snooze in the sun if conditions are right.

It is not a bad idea to take the boots off again and walk about barefoot, ground permitting. Some even carry a pair of lightweight moccasins for such moments. After all, it is your first time out and the pursuit is intended to be pleasurable. There is no point in pushing yourself prematurely. You may already consider yourself in training for the Big One, next year or whenever, but let the acclimatizing and bodily conditioning come progressively and reasonably painlessly.

If you have paced yourself properly the boots should be pulled on again and the pack hoisted without too many groans. You will no doubt have chatted to the publican or locals about your final destination and will have a fair idea just how far that is and what the prospects ahead are like.

Ideally, it should not be much further than 3 to 5 miles distant, depending on age and aptitude, and your penultimate rest stop should be at the village where you intend to

Even the most determined backpackers sometimes resort to the bus shelters in conditions like this

pick up your food supply for the evening meal and next morning's breakfast.

We must assume it is not Sunday or half-day closing (you very soon learn to be not only weather-conscious but shop-hour conscious too, as a backpacker). Do not leave it too late; 5.00 p.m. is often shutter-closing time in rural Britain. On the credit side, even the smallest stores now have freezer cabinets full of convenience foods and, whilst the contents may be a bit plastic, calorie value is unaffected.

Of course, you may get lucky and stumble on one of those old-fashioned family butchers or a store that carries ham on the bone and other goodies. Whatever you find, you will just have to manage. Flexibility and a stoic acceptance of whatever's on offer is something else you quickly learn as a self-reliant independent traveller. And there is nothing shameful in having a café or restaurant meal occasionally; especially if it is pelting with rain, the shops are closed and your spirits low. But you should also be able to tighten your belt and make do with those iron rations in the pack if you have to. In any case, it is all part of the fun to play it by ear.

On the first day, though, we will assume all is sweetness and light. Those precious victuals are safely in the pack – or, if there is no room, in a stuff-sack used as a shopping bag and carried that way for the final mile or so. One sensible rule to observe in what might be termed populated backpacking country: only buy what you need immediately. Tomorrow is another day and you hardly want to spend it walking with a pack suddenly larger and heavier than it was when you started.

Over the last hill then, down to some sheltered and secluded spot where you are destined to spend that first night under the stars. There may be a detectable tiredness across the shoulders, perhaps a little tenderness in the hip-belt region, and more than likely your feet will be trying to tell you something.

Above all, however, you *should* feel a quite distinct physical satisfaction – maybe even tinged with elation. You are possibly 12 to 15 miles from where you started out, you have navigated the path properly and you have done it under your own steam. It is a feeling better experienced than described.

Chapter Six
Pitching Camp

As you will quickly discover, the backpacker enjoys something of a special relationship with the rural community. You get a seal of approval for arriving on foot, as opposed to invading by car. Appreciable nods of welcome and friendly assistance will be commonplace in smaller villages and hamlets.

Responsible behaviour is essential, however, to maintain this happy alliance between countryside residents and visiting pedestrians. Muddy boots on pub carpets, packs swinging destructively in cluttered village stores and tent pitching without permission, make for disapproval, if not hostility.

The unwritten rules are not hard to obey; indeed, they are automatically followed by all those with a modicum of common sense and awareness of the country code, particularly when it comes to overnight pitching.

Never forget that every acre of land in Britain is owned by someone. You cannot pitch your tent on common land, national park, or anywhere else *as a right*. Permission, on the other hand, is not hard to obtain, especially for a small lightweight tent (sometimes known as a 'pup' tent), and will usually be given freely, if sought.

Sometimes, it must be conceded, this is not possible. Then you must be circumspect, reasonable and ready to pack and go voluntarily if confronted by a landowner, bailiff or other guardian of the terrain. By way of encouragement, I would just mention that, in many years of lightweight travel, I have never yet been rejected or ejected, nor have any of my friends or acquaintances. Diplomacy

In Scotland. This looks like an ideal position to camp, but permission should always be sought from the landowner

coupled with a responsible attitude should ensure the same for you.

So let us say you have spied a likely pitch, gained permission from the farm house and are ready to go to ground. What then is the immediate sequence of activity? The first is to find a level, sheltered patch of ground and one that will not be instantly swamped if the heavens open.

It is always worthwhile spending a few minutes deciding on your position, even if you are dog tired. It pays to pitch on *slightly* rising ground, close to a natural windbreak like a haystack, stone wall, stand of trees or even a fold in the terrain in open country. The object, always, is to dodge the worst of any prevailing wind.

If the wind is piping strongly, stroll around for a bit, pausing here and there, to find the least affected area. It is surprising sometimes what a difference a yard or two can make. Avoid water-trap hollows – very soft earth or too-lush grass – and any pitch directly beneath large trees, especially elm. Young conifers or feathery birch are safe enough, but remember if a storm breaks the drips will plop irritatingly on the flysheet long after the rain has stopped. Open sky immediately overhead is favourable.

If you have picked a benign weather spell, the morning dew may well be heavy. So try to position your tent so it will benefit from the sunrise. It is always pleasing to wake under those first warming rays and you will also have the satisfaction of packing the tent dry.

If the chosen patch of ground is level, so much the better but if, as often happens, the ground slopes, make sure you pitch the tent for a head-up sleeping position. Lastly, before setting up, make sure there are no jagged flints or obvious groundsheet tearers lying in

65

wait. Use your knife to prize out any suspicious debris. Stomping a depression in the earth where you think your hip and shoulder will end up is optional, as is collecting armfuls of bracken or dead leaves to pad the sleeping area. For a super-soft bed you need an air mattress, but more on this in the next chapter.

The actual pitching of the tent should pose no problems if you have carried out that home-lawn dry run. Standard procedure is to lay out the inner compartment (zip door closed), and peg out the four groundsheet corners. Just lift the inner material to check that it is nicely taut with no marked ruckles. This will confirm that you have positioned the unit squarely, thus putting subsequent strain on all seams, zips and pole locating points at a minimum.

Poles come next and with most models these are set up from the outside. If you do have to crawl inside to fix the rear one, watch that your boots do not plaster the inner with mud or, worse, snag the material. Set the inner tent *reasonably* firmly though not enough to strain the zip door. Wait until the flysheet is thrown over and secured and only then go around retightening (or repositioning if necessary) all pegs and guylines.

With both the inner tent and the flysheet always peg the main holding points first. That is to say, the four corners of the inner, the front and rear of the flysheet, and then the four corners. Leave the intermediate pegs until last or you will never achieve that desirable wrinkle-free, tailored look so essential if rain is to be shed efficiently and flapping to be avoided during high winds.

With the final pegging down of the flysheet you can be quite firm (though never brutal), for the material and fixing points are considerably tougher than they might appear. Push all the pegs well into the ground, then attach inner tent walls to flysheet if links are provided, open the zip doorway, and your nylon lair is ready for furnishing and occupation.

At this stage, secure in the knowledge that even if a storm breaks it will not matter much, most of us now pause in our labours to enjoy a drink and a stretch, sorting the night gear,

Walkers often have access to camp sites which are closed to cars
Right: *On with the outer tent and* (below) *pitched and ready to unpack after a day's walk*

food supply and completing camp chores at a very leisurely pace – chores like filling the water bag, for example, which is usually the first and most important requirement. With the $2\frac{1}{2}$ gallon unit recommended, you should have ample water for one night, including that needed for washing, shaving or making up any freeze-dried foods. So a stroll to the farm house is a once only, not too arduous, task.

If your backpacking day has gone as it should, you will be not merely hungry, but famished. And no food tastes so good as that cooked and eaten in the open air. But you have to adopt some sort of system to enjoy it to the full.

It is a question of getting the sequence right, with just one burner ring at your disposal and a distinctly limited range of utensils.

Camping by a site table adds a touch of luxury

Any hot meal should be *hot* and there are two
basic ways in which the backpacker ensures
this: by eating each dish as it is cooked; or by
using that very handy kitchen foil (standard
wrapping of Chinese takeaways) to keep any
secondary dishes steaming. With practice, you
can produce a variety of gourmet menus using
silver foil. On the other hand, you may be
quite content, on this maiden voyage at least,
to tuck away something quick and simple like
a large T-bone steak.

Whatever the meal, adopt the habit of
cleaning up as you go along. The crack of
dawn is no time to face dirty pots and pans.
In any case this is a sloppy expedition practice.
Every item in the outfit should be kept clean,
bright and ready for use. This way *you* stay
clean, comfortable and efficient. A tiny bottle
of liquid soap, a J-cloth and one of those small
abrasive pads is the standard mini cleaning
kit.

Evening activity may be a meander to the
nearest pub (if reserves of energy permit), or
a lounge around camp and perhaps a nightcap.
Whatever, you will find that the time between
shedding your pack after the day's walk and
the irresistible call of the sleeping bag will
pass surprisingly quickly.

Just before you turn in, though, check the
tent pegs and guylines and make sure that the
separation of flysheet and inner tent is as it
should be. If the dusk dew is heavy, it may be
necessary to readjust tautness of the nylon
flysheet which, though not affected to anything
like the same degree as cotton canvas, can sag
slightly in damp air. If your empty pack is
left in the open, make sure it stays dry by
covering it with a plastic liner.

In preparing for bed the degree of undressing depends largely on personal preference and prevailing conditions. The only criterion is snug warmth. Just as one adjusts clothing for comfortable walking, so one sheds or dons garments before getting into the sleeping bag according to the climate.

You may be happy to sleep naked if your pitch is along some stretch of Devon footpath in high summer. At 3000 feet in the Cairngorms in late autumn, on the other hand, you will probably find yourself wearing more clothing at night than you are during the day. Pyjamas are a wasteful luxury, though some are prepared to pack a tracksuit which doubles as night attire and for general wear around camp.

So, with the canteen of water filled for early morning tea, the matches stowed dry where you can find them easily, and the torch

You are never too young to start backpacking and it can become a lifetime's pleasure

handily placed, you are all set to call it a day. Do not expect to sleep as soundly as you do at home, though.

Unless you are one of those rare beings who can sleep anywhere, the first night will probably be a fitful one and, despite physical tiredness, you may not drop off really deeply until first light. This is usual and nothing to worry about.

It gets better with repetition, as the body adjusts to outdoor living and the mind becomes attuned to the night sounds of nature. For comfort, remember you are reverting in some ways to sleeping much as our ancestors did – not exactly with one eye open, but certainly with those primeval instincts reawakened. Eight hours unbroken oblivion

on a spring mattress, pampered by central heating, was hardly their style.

Surprisingly, you will not feel drowsy for very long next morning. By the time you have washed, breakfasted, broken camp and hoisted your pack, you should be fully alert with any night restlessness already forgotten. As I said, it gets better with practice.

At this time, with the dawn mist still swirling, so to speak, the subject of natural function is perhaps timely. Natural is the operative word and no inhibitions should prevent your normal routine. Just take the toilet roll, walk into the woods, and bear in mind that other admirable tenet of the back-packer: leave no mark in passing.

All soluble waste should be buried and this of course includes that generated by camping overnight: food scraps, paper, cigarette ends and so forth. Empty tins and plastic bags on the other hand should *not* be interred where there are farm animals. Cattle are curious and they are too valuable to injure with jagged tins or choke with plastic.

You arrived with the items, after all, so if in any doubt bag them up, replace in the pack and jettison later in an appropriate rubbish container. Empty food tins stamped flat and wrapped in plastic take up little temporary room in the backpack. Doing your social duty thus should give you a feeling of virtue.

A last look around your overnight pitch should – indeed must, in the interest of the whole fraternity – reveal nothing more tell-tale than a patch of flattened grass. A double check is a good idea too, just to make sure you have not left a towel hanging on a tree branch (or even that precious water bag), or some smaller, equally valuable item, half hidden in the grass.

A parting word of thanks to the farmer, if practicable, is a normal courtesy and should ensure that future backpackers will be welcomed as you were; especially when it is seen that you have left the landscape as you found it.

Top left: *Loading up in the morning*
Left: *There's room to make quite a comfortable mess in even a small tent*

Chapter Seven
A Step Further

So far – and rightly, since this is an introductory book – concentration has been upon basic backpacking, that is the essential items of equipment and a gentle, fair-weather introduction to technique. No introduction, however should be entirely elementary and since, sooner or later, you will assuredly be tempted to try the sterner stuff, this chapter is devoted to more advanced backpacking – the best kind there is in the opinion of many seasoned veterans.

For these hardened types, the season does not even *begin* until late October when the swallows have flown, the night air is crisp and hoar frosts herald the mornings. It is a heady time of year, when the countryside is quieter, the walking invigorating and the challenge of combating the elements real and exciting, especially on high-level routes.

To play the winter game, though, there are a number of cardinal rules that must be observed to ensure you do not put yourself – or others – in jeopardy. For a start at least, do not be tempted to go solo in high country. A team of two is satisfactory (provided one is reasonably experienced), three even better.

The rules about safety in the hills are clearly laid down and readily available at all the recognized climbing and hill-walking centres in Great Britain. Read, digest and act upon them intelligently to avoid becoming an unfortunate newspaper statistic.

Amongst the more obvious self-imposed disciplines are those that decree you do not tackle any high-level route in obviously deteriorating weather; that you unfailingly leave notice about your itinerary and approximate timing – even if this is merely a note on

Winter backpacking in the Lakes

the car windscreen – and that if you *are* caught out you know precisely what to do. You do not, for example, rush in panic down to valley level (the route to hypothermia rather than a haven), but hole up snugly and patiently until conditions improve.

Which brings us naturally to the predominant concern of winter backpacking: keeping warm. No marks for guessing that this means a further financial outlay and a consequently heavier backpack. The requirements are threefold: protective warmth when walking and when static, plus inner warmth via an increase of calorie intake.

The last is very important, and can cause a vicious circle. The colder the climate and the heavier the pack, the more energy expended. The more you need to stoke up inwardly the more food that must be carried. All very tricky.

The answer is to pace oneself carefully, keeping the daily mileage well within personal maximum and making sure supplies consist of high-protein food which is not too bulky, such as corned beef, bars of chocolate, Kendal Mint Cake and concentrated soup.

Even if you do not realize it mentally, your body will soon tell you that a winter trek along a moorland hill-top route means an enormous energy output. Your need to feed heartily will become urgent, if not desperate. So heed the signals and act accordingly. Some manage with a little-and-often system, others favour a gargantuan feast at the end of each day. Your own metabolism will dictate which is preferred.

Whatever the choice, the end result is the same – an increase of pack weight from a modest 20 pound summer load to 35 pounds or more by dint of extra clothing, food and bedding. It follows then that everyone who attempts advanced backpacking should be in reasonable physical shape, reasonably experienced and totally familiar with his or her equipment.

The summer sport will go a long way towards building up fitness and increasing your knowledge, especially if trips are made frequently with a gentle increase of miles walked and weight carried. Getting into shape is a very rewarding challenge in itself and need not in any way be arduous if personal potential is stretched progressively and gradually.

As expertise increases, so will confidence and the healthy tendency towards self-criticism. Any problems with technique or equipment will be ironed out almost unconsciously by experience. You may, for instance, discover that a patch of moleskin (medicinal not animal despite the name) is the perfect cure for some persistent foot hot-spot. That swatting up on map and compass work (vital to all wanderers from the beaten track) pays big dividends – if you keep as near as possible to the same contour you will traverse any high level route the easy way, rather than zig-zagging up and down hill.

So, although the pack may be heavier in more advanced backpacking, your improved physical condition and native cunning will do much to offset this. Remember too that, within reason, the colder the climate the more comfortable you will be walking with a pack. Countless numbers of enthusiasts manage to cope with the extra loading, and so, after a while, will you.

Winter extras are usually those needed for combating night cold, and the prime requirement here is to escape immediate contact with the ground. This the Karrimat ensures and nothing, as already stated, is more efficient. It does not do much to soften the earth, however, which can be iron hard during the darker months.

So a word in favour of the air mattress, particularly for those in the middle years whose bones may not be quite so flexible as they once were. Personally, I find it makes an enormous difference to sleeping comfort. So much so that the extra pack weight is worthwhile even in summer.

Choosing the right air bed is important, though, for many are far too heavy and bulky to be considered. My own choice is the Austrian Semperit nylon waffle pattern. This is a full-length unit with attached pillow; acceptably lightweight at $1\frac{3}{4}$ pounds, it packs down very small and is tough enough to give years of reliable service.

This must of course be supplemented with a Karrimat, since any air bed alone is virtually as cold as the ground it is laid upon. In order to keep the full bed-roll within practical limits, a short length of the 3 millimetre is perfectly adequate. This combination makes for a warm, luxuriously pneumatic underlay.

Hip-length air beds, or combination sleeping mats of close-cell foam and inflatable sections, find favour with some backpackers. One or two, mainly American, actually self-inflate via a screw valve. Some are better than others, but all are somewhat slim and spartan with a weight/bulk factor only fractionally less than the full-sized unit described.

In deep winter there is nothing to compare with the four-season, down-filled mountaineering sleeping bag. The cost though is somewhat frightening and the bulk is positively prohibitive when compared with the middle-range bags. Unless you intend a winter assault on the Eiger, there are alternatives nearly as efficient and a lot cheaper.

One method is to sleeve the main sleeping bag with a lightweight version either bought specially for summer use or made up from an old domestic eiderdown. Another is to treat yourself to a duvet waistcoat or full jacket. Excellent dual-purpose garments these, since they are also ideal for daytime rest wear.

The third way of ensuring full body warmth is to invest in a two-piece thermal undersuit like the Norwegian Helly Hanson. It is quite expensive, but very efficient, long lasting and comfortable to wear day or night.

Supplementary heating once inside the tent may be supplied by a charcoal burning hand-warmer. Stowed inside the sleeping bag, this will provide up to six hours extra heating from

Falls in the Lake District . . .

. . . But a sharp landlord corners the route

a single stick of charcoal. If you wish to read, well the flame from a sterine candle will also warm a pup tent interior quite efficiently and for a long time. Just make sure it is positioned safely. After this, whatever disturbs your sleep, it should not be the cold night air.

Winter backpacking demands that daytime clothing be more substantial than the summer variety. Thermal underwear perhaps, more pullovers, and for lower-limb warmth a pair of backpacking trousers in Derby tweed material. These are excellent, being very hard wearing and warm, even when wet. They are more popular than the shorter climbing breeches with most backpackers.

For the all-important extremities, there are 'hot socks' (very soft and thick lambs wool), or loop-stitch socks either ankle length or knee length. Dachstein oiled-wool mittens keep the hands protected against the iciest wind and they remain fairly impervious to wet for a long time. Waterproof overmitts are useful during heavy and prolonged rain.

The standard headgear in winter is the balaclava helmet. The genuine article, made from 100 per cent pure wool, is superbly warm and windproof and it can be worn at night with the neck protector and face mask pulled down, and during the day as an orthodox hat.

The natural inclination, once the kit additions for more advanced backpacking have been completed, is to try them out under field conditions. Proceed slowly though, for rough-country travel in winter is very different from those benign stretches of valley footpath in summer.

It may be at this stage that you feel the need to seek further encouragement from those with first-hand experience. Here, whilst declaring something of a vested interest, I must commend you to the Backpackers Club, which exists expressly to promote, sustain and widen the interests of all independent foot travellers.

Amongst the benefits – apart from meeting like-minded contemporaries – are the *Farm Pitch Directory*, which contains a list of many secluded farms nationwide where backpackers are welcome, and access to parts of Forestry Commission terrain.

County groups, each with their own co-ordinator, exist to help the newcomer; there is a bi-monthly magazine called *Backchat*, a lending library of useful maps and pertinent books and a calendar of events. There is also a discount scheme for members operated by a number of specialist retailers throughout the country.

Every backpack takes on a character of its own

Dubbed the 'the club for unclubbables', there are no committees, a delightful dearth of written rules and you can remain as anti-social as you wish. Indeed, this is one club where going your own way is a positive virtue. Newcomers gain experience very quickly; they also widen their options and strike up new friendships. There is a Young Backpackers Section for juveniles.

As experience brings expertise, the high and lonely places in these islands may beckon more and more. Like climbing, backpacking can become a drug difficult to live without. Those of us who are addicts know the unique exhilaration of crossing those rocky paths, half in, half out of the clouds, the solitary but never lonely delight, and the workaday world left far below. The sense of well-being and complete independence which backpacking provides is appreciated to the full at such times. Come daylight or darkness, fair weather or foul, we have the wherewithal to cope and it is all in that snug-fitting shoulder load. Self-reliance does not come in any better form.

With just a little luck we can continue to tramp the high-level tracks into old age (indeed the more we do the more likely we are to reach old age in a healthy and strong condition) with scarcely an anxious moment if we practise our sport with prudence.

Nature, however, can turn hostile alarmingly quickly at altitude and even the most experienced can be caught out sometimes. The emergency drill on such occasions (when a white-out occurs, for instance, through a sudden descent of mist, rain, sleet or snow) is admirably expressed in concise Yorkshire dialect: 'When in doubt, do nowt.'

Never attempt to race the weather down to valley level, temptingly near though it may seem. Stay on the path, pitch the tent, cocoon yourself and wait. If the hold-up is caused through personal injury, like a twisted ankle, the routine is the same. Keep calm, stay put and, if you cannot see, do not go.

Others will find you eventually, so long as you left word as you should have done at the starting point. Secure in this knowledge, you are nine-tenths towards overcoming the greatest danger of the emergency: fear of fear itself.

It may never happen, of course, but, just in case, *always* carry a small but comprehensive first-aid kit and the basic items of survival in mountain country, like high-protein iron rations, whistle and torch. Thus armed, you can sustain yourself for a long time if needs be, then signal audibly or visually to the help which will finally and *assuredly* arrive.

77

Chapter Eight
Trailblazing in Britain and abroad

Despite heavy overpopulation and the steady incursion of concrete into this green and pleasant land, Britain is still one of the best walking countries in the world. We who back-pack are – or should be – eternally grateful for such a diversity of footpaths, landscapes and (despite grumbles) a climate that is truly temperate – all within a tiny land mass.

Further, we have government, both national and regional, committed to preserving and improving access to the countryside where possible and this includes a vast network of footpaths criss-crossing national parks and other areas designated as of outstanding natural beauty.

One official body largely responsible for maintaining this happy state of affairs is the Countryside Commission, who publish very useful literature, some of which is free, on all the major long-distance footpath routes. This is obtainable either directly (see Useful Addresses, page 89), or from local tourist offices. Thus, for the first long expedition, you can choose a path not too arduous and geographically suitable.

One such is the South Downs Way, an interesting 80 miles of Sussex downland that winds continuously from Beachy Head to the Hampshire border above Chichester Harbour. Steeped in history, with many high spots along the way like the Long Man of Wilmington and Chanctonbury Ring, it has practical assets too.

Left: *At the end of the day's walk good cooking equipment is really appreciated*
Overleaf: *The South Downs way, showing youth hostels, villages and places of interest. Maps of all the National Trust footpaths are available from the Countryside Commission*

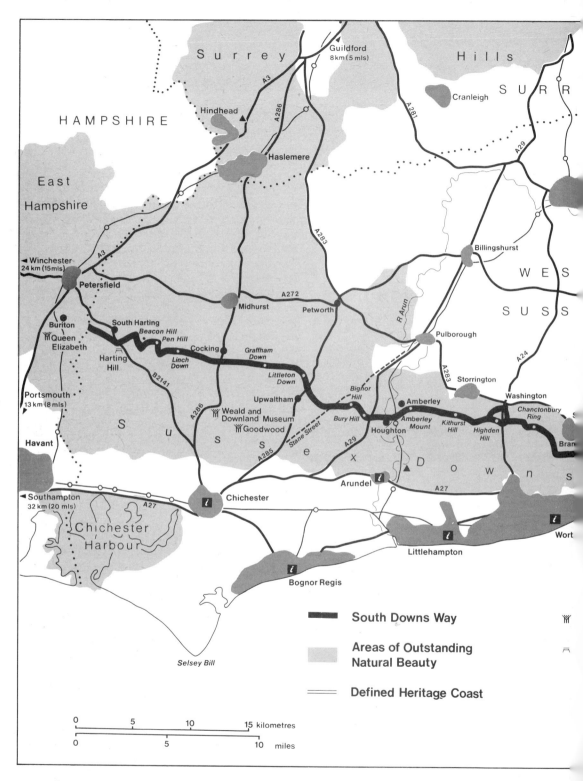

South Downs Way

Areas of Outstanding Natural Beauty

Defined Heritage Coast

```
0        5        10       15 kilometres
0             5              10  miles
```

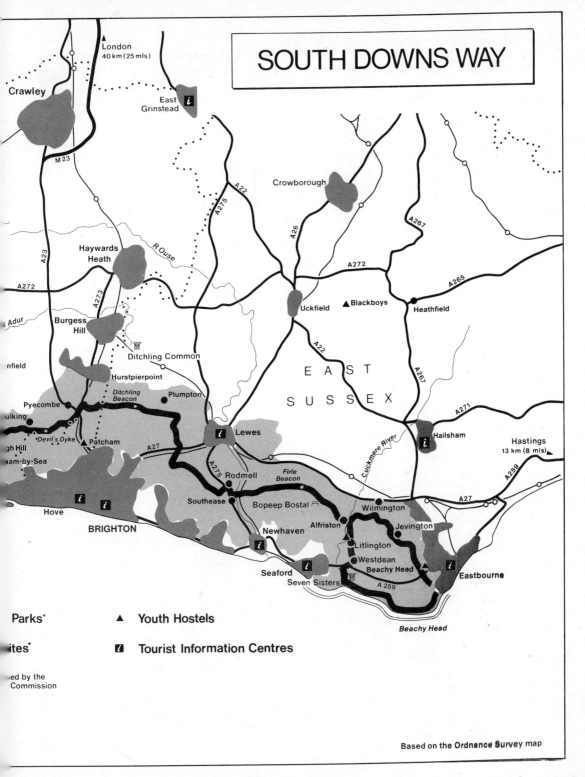

SOUTH DOWNS WAY

London
40 km (25 mls)

Crawley

East
Grinstead

M 23

Crowborough

A22

A275

A26

A267

Haywards
Heath

R Ouse

A23

A272

A272

A265

Adur

Burgess
Hill

Uckfield

▲ Blackboys

Heathfield

A273

Ditchling Common

E A S T

A22

A267

nfield

Hurstpierpoint

S U S S E X

Ditchling
Beacon

Plumpton

A271

Pyecombe

Cuckmere River

Hailsham

Hastings
13 km (8 mls) ▲

ulking

Devil's Dyke

▲ Patcham

A27

Lewes

gh Hill

A275

Rodmell

Firle
Beacon

A259

am-by-Sea

A27

Hove

Southease

Bopeep Bostal

Wilmington

Jevington

BRIGHTON

Newhaven

Alfriston

Litlington

Westdean
Beachy Head

Eastbourne

Seaford

Seven Sisters

A 259

Beachy Head

Parks*

▲ **Youth Hostels**

ites*

i **Tourist Information Centres**

ed by the
Commission

Based on the Ordnance Survey map

Though largely a high-level route, it is of a gentle height, and the path is perfectly defined along the chalk-down ridge – which eliminates a lot of map and compass work. Descent to valley level is easy and hamlets and small towns are closely spaced. A good initiation route this and, for those wishing to walk it, the booklet entitled *Along the South Downs Way* (obtainable locally and moderately priced) is a knowledgeable step-by-step guide.

The Berkshire Ridgeway, or more correctly the Ridgeway Path (since it traverses much more than this one county), is another popular southern route. It begins at Ivinghoe Beacon near Dunstable and runs for some 85 miles through five counties to the ancient Avebury Stone Circle in Wiltshire. The latter stretch particularly, through the Vale of the White Horse, is one of great open-country, open-sky beauty.

Further west, the New Forest, administered by the pro-backpacking Forestry Commission, holds appeal, particularly for newcomers, since it offers relatively low-level walking over well-defined paths through a mainly tree-sheltered landscape. There is a variety of circular forest and heathland trails here, linked by Commission camp grounds where special areas are set aside for pedestrian lightweight campers.

Not far from here, at the western end of Poole Harbour, begins the longest continuous trail in Britain: the South-West Peninsula Path. Now broken into four sections, this is a real marathon, effectively following the entire south-west peninsula of England from Poole in Dorset to Minehead in Somerset – some 515 miles.

It is a rugged, often regal, coastline, punctuated by scenic gems like Lulworth Cove, Golden Cap (highest point on the south coast), Start Point and Polperro, that film-set fishing harbour of southern Cornwall. Between Padstow and Bude is one of the most beautiful sections of coast path in Britain, whilst that around North Devon and across Somerset to the finish at Minehead is only slightly less dramatic.

Another favoured route in the south, close to London, is the North Downs Way, 140 miles of Kent and Surrey hills which start at Farnham and finish at Dover. This path coincides in parts with the famous Pilgrims' Way, of which Canterbury and its magnificent cathedral was the great historical objective.

All these paths are suitable for beginners.

Wales has two particularly fine long-distance routes: Offa's Dyke and the Pembrokeshire Coast Path, and here we come to backpacking for the experienced. Offa's Dyke for instance, is strenuous and requires efficient map reading and compass work, and the high sections of moorland and mountain can be hostile in rough weather.

Notwithstanding, it is a magnificent 170 miles of wild grandeur, running the entire length of the border between England and Wales, from Chepstow to Prestatyn. Named after the mysterious eighth-century King of Mercia, the path still traces the line of the mighty earthworks, where possible. A route of contrast, it ranges from the lush valleys of the Wye to the open sweeps of the Brecon Beacons and remote ruggedness of the Clwydian range above Llangollen.

Corfe Castle

The Pembrokeshire path is easier to follow since it traces the coastline. Scenically impressive, though somewhat fragmented in parts and fairly heavy going, the path itself is often overgrown and ill defined. Some sections are difficult, even hazardous, and should only be tackled by the really fit. Fine for those who love a challenge, though, sparsely populated for the most part and one of the richest areas for seabirds in the British Isles.

The Pennine Way takes pride of place as the most romantic long-distance footpath in Britain. Not the longest, but the first to be opened officially (largely through the tireless efforts of one man, Tom Stephenson), it is the toughest of them all and the most rewarding to walk.

240 miles of challenging terrain along the very spine of England, starting in Derbyshire at the foot of mighty Kinder Scout and finishing at the erstwhile gypsy encampment, Kirk Yetholm, just over the border in Scotland. It is almost obligatory for every backpacker worthy of the name, to tackle the Way at some time. Proof of its magnetism can be seen in the steady increase of foot traffic which grows with every year that passes.

Thankfully, there is, so far, room for all. The start, around Edale, suffers a heavy influx of visitors during summer, but the serious walker very soon leaves the throng behind. In the main, the high-level path winds through a *still* largely secret Britain, amid scenery that is always dramatic, often breathtaking.

High spots along the route include Kinder Downfall, Malham Cove, Keld, High Cup Nick, Hadrian's Wall and the Cheviots, to name only a few. Walking time is anything from two to three weeks depending on season, personal fitness and size of backpack.

Lightweight 'wild' camping along this and the other paths mentioned poses few problems, especially along the less-frequented stretches. Do bear in mind, though, that those precious rights of way granted to walkers also entail responsibility, as outlined in the last chapter.

Top left: *Kimmeridge, Dorset*
Left: *On the South-West Peninsula Path*

There are strategically placed official camp grounds, mostly on farms, along the inland routes, more numerous and with holiday camping park alternatives along coastal paths. There is no reason why the backpacker should not take advantage of these official pitches from time to time, particularly if the facilities include hot showers and a laundry room. There is no virtue in being slavishly spartan. Most of us even succumb to the welcome warmth of a pub bed and breakfast occasionally, when weather conditions are particularly horrific. And why not, in the interest of variety?

Of course, it is not necessary to commit yourself to a long-distance footpath. The New Forest, already mentioned, is just one of the attractive backpacking areas of Britain where you can walk a pre-planned circular route lasting a weekend or three weeks. The Lake District National Park is equally popular but likely to be just as crowded in the summer as the New Forest. Backpackers, along with other pedestrian visitors, are the only ones who can really escape the crowds in either of these highly populated playgrounds during July and August.

Snowdonia National Park has its devotees too, particularly those who like to mix walking with rock scrambling or climbing; the Yorkshire Moors have appeal for distance walkers with lots of stamina; whilst parts of Scotland offer some of the best backpacking in Britain in the opinion of many. The Cairngorm Mountains around Aviemore are one magnet, Galloway Forest Park – the Highlands in miniature – in south-west Scotland, another.

All these, with the exception of the New Forest, are really the province of the experienced and should not be tackled solo whilst you remain in the novice stage. Suitable training areas abound in Britain and there are countless places where you can spread your backpacking wings.

The Cotswolds, Chilterns, Thetford Forest in Norfolk, Dovedale in Derbyshire, the Mendips, the Surrey Hills and endless miles of coastal path, all provide scenic and safe terrain where you can progressively perfect the art of self-reliant, self-contained travel. There

85

The Llairgh Ghru path from Aviemore to Braemar

High Cup Nick on the Pennine Way

is sufficient countryside worth exploring within these islands of ours to last a lifetime.

Being the restless creature he is, however, the backpacker may eventually be tempted to roam further afield. After all, the world really is his oyster and the lure of foreign fields may exert an irresistible pull in due course.

So far as Europe is concerned, there is no question that Switzerland is the supreme backpacking country for any enthusiast making his first foray outside Britain. Never mind the criticisms about its being too clinically clean, dull and impossibly expensive. It also

has some of the most majestic mountains in the world, all concentrated within a small area, plus a footpath network that is probably unequalled anywhere. A unique double blessing for the walker.

Comprehensive and meticulously accurate literature enables you to plan a backpacking trip through this icing-sugar landscape, knowing that all information about distances and terrain and the walking times (in hours *and* minutes), will be precise.

It may not offer all the excitement of the unknown, but Switzerland is a first-class

Falcon Clints on the Pennine Way

introduction to foreign foot travel. There are some spectacular long-distance paths, with camping grounds and villages closely spaced. You can expect high standards of honesty and social behaviour, English is one of the *lingua francas* and, provided you eat modestly – mainly in camp – and keep well away from ski lifts and the like, it is not ruinously expensive. A springtime trip through the Swiss Alps will, given a little luck with the weather, be as memorable as any you are ever likely to make.

And after Switzerland? The Dordogne, Auvergne or Tarn Gorges of France perhaps, Germany's Black Forest, the Pyrenees, Dolomites, Sweden's Kingsway Trail or that marvellous route from the English Channel to the Mediterranean. And, who knows, you may even find yourself setting foot one day upon the mighty Appalachian Trail in North America. At which stage you will be far too knowledgeable for any beginner's guide like this. Good walking!

Appendix 1:
Further Reading

Appendix 2:
Useful Addresses

The Backpackers Handbook by Derek Booth
(Robert Hale)
Backpacking in Britain by Robin Adshead
and Derek Booth (Oxford Illustrated Press)
Teach Yourself Backpacking by Peter Lumley
(Teach Yourself Books)
Journey Through Britain by John Hillaby,
President, Backpackers Club (Paladin)
Backpacking, a Comprehensive Guide by
Showell Styles (Macmillan)
Spur Book of Map & Compass by Terry
Brown and Rob Hunter (Spur)

Magazines
Practical Camper (Haymarket Press)
Great Outdoors (Holmes McDougall)
Climber & Rambler (Holmes McDougall)
Camping (Link House)

Countryside Commission, John Dower House,
Crescent Place, Cheltenham, Gloucestershire
GL50 3RA (*Free leaflets with maps of
Britain's long-distance paths, plus guidebooks.
SAE advisable.*)

Backpackers Club, 20 St Michael's Road,
Tilehurst Road, Reading, Berkshire RG3 4RP
(*National Organizer Eric Gurney. SAE
essential.*)

Camping Club of Great Britain and Ireland
Ltd, 11 Grosvenor Place, London SW1W 0EY
(*Britain's oldest and most respected outdoor-
life club has a special section for lightweight
campers.*) Northern address: Camping Club of
Great Britain (Association of Cycle and
Lightweight Campers), 22 Holmsley Field
Lane, Oulton, Leeds, Yorkshire

Blacks of Greenock, Port Glasgow, Scotland

Banton & Co. Ltd (Pointfive), Meadow Lane,
Nottingham NG2 3HP

Berghaus Ltd, 34 Dean Street, Newcastle-
upon-Tyne

Karrimor International Ltd, Avenue Parade,
Accrington, Lancashire

Robert Saunders Ltd, Five Oaks Lane,
Chigwell, Essex

Helly-Hansen (UK) Ltd, Ronald Close,
Kempston, Bedfordshire MK42 7SJ